IT'S GOOD TO BE
ALIVE

IT'S GOOD TO BE ALIVE

OBSERVATIONS FROM A WHEELCHAIR

JACK RUSHTON

Bonneville Books
Springville, Utah

ISBN 13: 978-1-59955-408-2

Published by Bonneville Books, an imprint of Cedar Fort, Inc.
2373 W. 700 S., Springville, UT 84663
Distributed by Cedar Fort, Inc., www.cedarfort.com

Library of Congress Cataloging-in-Publication Data

    Rushton, Jack L. (Jack Louis), 1938-
    It's good to be alive : observations from a wheelchair / Jack L. Rushton.
      p. cm.
    Summary: Autobiography of Jack Rushton, who at age 50 was in a surfing accident and paralyzed from the neck down.
    ISBN 978-1-59955-408-2
    1. Rushton, Jack L. (Jack Louis), 1938– 2. Mormons—California--Biography. 3. People with disabilities—California—Biography. 4. Paralytics—California—Biography. 5. Autobiographies—Mormon authors. I. Title.

    HV3013.R87 A3 2010
    362.4'3092--dc22
    [B]

2010012371

Cover design by Danie Romrell
Cover design © 2010 by Lyle Mortimer
Typeset by Melissa J. Caldwell
Edited by Kimiko Christensen Hammari

Printed in the United States of America

10 9 8 7 6 5 4 3 2 1

Printed on acid-free paper

To Jo Anne

Contents

Introduction

CALIFORNIA BEACHES ARE beautiful. Tuesday, August 1, 1989, was an especially bright, sunny day at Laguna Beach. The water was warm and the waves were not at all threatening. I was vacationing with my wife, Jo Anne, and three of our six children. Loaded down with baskets and blankets, we found a good spot in the sand without too many people around.

As my sixteen-year-old son, John, and his friend, Matt Mecuro, played in the ocean, JoAnne rubbed me down with sunscreen. The water was so tempting. I was really looking forward to body surfing with the boys. After thanking Jo Anne, I glanced over at my two youngest daughters, Rachel (age nine) and Jackie (age three), playing in the sand. Then I ran into the surf.

Just the Saturday night before, we'd held John's Eagle Court of Honor ceremony. Jo Anne had taken a picture of John and me standing next to each other in our scout

The last picture taken of Jack
before his accident.

uniforms. In fact, about a year later, John wrote a school
paper about what happened on the beach that fateful day. He
titled it "The Last Photograph" because, as he explains in
his paper, "It was the last picture taken of my father before
he became a quadriplegic." Little did I realize that night,
posing for a picture with my youngest son, that he would be
instrumental in saving my life a few days later.

Although we were having a great time riding the waves
that day, the boys wanted to get out and have some lunch.
We decided we would take one more ride into shore. I stood
next to John, waiting for the wave to come. When it did,

we both caught it perfectly. John pulled out before it became too shallow, but I was having such a good ride that I decided to take it all the way into the shore. Suddenly, my head hit a submerged rock. I immediately knew something was wrong because I couldn't move my arms or legs. Then swirling green sea water devoured me as I blacked out.

Thankfully, John saw me floating on top of the water, face down and not moving. With great effort, he and Matt were able to pull me onto the beach, where several teams of lifeguards did CPR until the paramedics arrived. Miraculously they were able to keep me alive. Two hours later I woke up in the hospital, surrounded by doctors and nurses.

I would later learn that the impact of the wave thrusting my head into the rock had broken my neck and severed my spinal column between the second and third cervical verte-brate. The nature of my injury is similar to that suffered by Christopher Reeve. I am paralyzed from the neck down and ventilator dependent.

My accident was initially devastating to me physically, spiritually, and emotionally. I was fifty years old at the time, had six children and two grandchildren, and was in my twenty-fifth year of working for my church's education system. It just didn't seem that life could get much better, and then, in one split second, the bottom dropped out. In the beginning, I did not see how I could go forward with my life, and making a quick exit didn't seem like such a bad idea.

In retrospect, it took almost five years to make the adjustments necessary to have the wonderful quality of life I enjoy now. With the passage of time, as my body stabilized and with the help of the Lord, I eventually made the adjustment from a "walking, normal person" to a quadriplegic operating a huge power wheelchair and living on life support.

One of my greatest fears after being paralyzed was the impact it would have on my family, especially my roles as husband, father, and grandfather. One early morning, many years ago, I was pondering the dilemma of how I might be more effective in these capacities. As I was lying in bed, waiting for Jo Anne to wake up and begin our day, an idea was born. A very strong impression came to me that perhaps I could have some influence for good upon my posterity through my writing. I could share with them my observations about life and I could do it all through email!

Up to that time, voice recognition software had been very rudimentary but was just beginning to take off, as was the quality of personal computers. This truly was something I could do! My first observations were family oriented, but my children, finding them humorous and even sometimes interesting and insightful, began sharing them with friends. Before long, more and more people expressed a desire to receive them, and the list has now grown to include many wonderful people from around the world. I sign off on each observation as "Dad/Grandpa/Jack."

Since that time, I have written more than two hundred

observations and plan to do more. I have no ax to grind. I just try to respond to current events in my life and also delve into history—personal, family, religious, and secular—all from the perspective of a quadriplegic on life support.

Having lived in two dimensions—"normal and walking" and then as part of a "disabled minority group"—I believe my observations are unique. Few people have been privileged to sit in my chair. I use the word *privileged* because I have been able to learn and experience things that wouldn't have been possible otherwise.

As I write this introduction, I am in the twenty-first year of my injury. I have lived to see sixteen more grandchildren join our family, making a total of eighteen. All but one of our children live within an hour's drive of our home in Tustin, California. Our oldest is a judge, while the others have careers as a schoolteacher, business owner, ER doctor, registered nurse, and music teacher. I am so grateful my life didn't end on the beach that day. I would have missed out on so much.

It's good to be alive—to be with JoAnne and all my family and good friends. I'm grateful I'm able to give service in my own unique way through writing, speaking, and

Jack and grandson Trevor Rushton

teaching. I'm grateful that as the years have passed, I have not become bitter or cynical. I am convinced that the challenging circumstances of life that come to all of us need not limit or control our behavior, preventing us from enjoying life. In fact, it is these very challenges that stretch us and help us grow in ways we never dreamed possible.

Jack L. Rushton

SECTION ONE

Life in a
WHEELCHAIR

I Wish It Was
YESTERDAY

WESTSIDE STORY HAS been one of my favorite Broadway musicals and films since 1962. In a rumble between rival gangs—the Jets and the Sharks—the leader of the Sharks was inadvertently stabbed to death by the leader of the Jets. The police came, the gang members all scattered, and later that night two of the Jets met up with one another. They were visibly shaken by what had happened, and in the ensuing conversation, one of the boys said, "I wish it was yesterday!" That haunting phrase, "I wish it was yesterday," always captures my attention. When I was lying in the hospital bed after my accident, I was not thinking of *West Side Story* and the phrase "I wish it was yesterday!" However, those words described my state of mind at that time perfectly.

Around midnight the head neurosurgeon sent all of my friends and family home so he could perform additional tests

The Rushton family in 1988, a year before Jack's accident.

to determine the extent of my injury. I have never felt more alone than I did when my loved ones departed that night. Yesterday had been beautiful as my family and I acted the part of tourists at the beach. Life couldn't have been better. There was not a cloud in the horizon of our lives, and it seemed like we would live happily ever after.

As I lay alone in the intensive care unit of the regional

trauma center that night, I could not believe what had happened to my family and me. How would we ever get through this tragedy? How would we survive financially? If I were permanently paralyzed, how on earth could I ever endure living this way? Those kinds of questions ran through my mind the entire night, and from the depths of my tortured soul, my heart cried out, "I wish it was yesterday!" I am sorry to report that I cried, "I wish it was yesterday" much longer than I would like to admit.

But the day finally came when I understood I could not be at peace or have a productive, meaningful life, unless I eliminated the phrase "I wish it was yesterday" from my vocabulary. That kind of thinking leads us nowhere.

Most of us have done something we have regretted or experienced a trial that has made us wish it was yesterday. How we would like to go back to the good old days before the tragic event took place. It is human nature to have that knee-jerk reaction to the challenges life can bring our way.

It has been so since the beginning of time. I wonder if Eve, as she gave birth to her first child, ever thought, "I wish it was yesterday" back in that beautiful garden.

Lot's wife was challenged as she looked back at Sodom with longing eyes and was turned into a pillar of salt—an inanimate object that could not act but could only be acted upon. She was unable to move forward; her progress came to an abrupt halt, which happens to all of us who live in the past.

The Rushton family in 2004.

Regardless of what may happen to us, we simply must press forward, never looking back. I no longer think, "I wish it was yesterday," for today is filled with joy and satisfaction.

Dad/Grandpa/Jack

My Name Is Jack—
I BROKE MY BACK

I BELIEVE ONE of the most frustrating and terrifying experiences a person can have is not being able to communicate, and as a result, not getting the help or reassurance needed to be comforted. The Lord gives babies the ability to cry, which is the only way they can communicate their needs. Though oftentimes annoying to adults, a baby's cry eventually gets adults' attention and is a vital tool of communication. Immediately following my accident, I couldn't speak at all and wasn't even able to cry out for help.

I was transported to the Mission Viejo Trauma Center by ambulance just hours after breaking my neck. It was nearly dark when the ambulance came to a stop outside the emergency area. The doors to the back of the ambulance swung open, and I was carefully lifted out on the gurney. As someone pushed, others walked beside me, carrying the apparatus that was pumping air into my lungs. I felt helpless and vulnerable laying flat on my back, unable to move or speak, and only seeing ceilings and faces.

The ICU seemed cold and sterile with all the hospital beds lined in a row, divided by curtains. My ears were sensitive to all the strange noises made by various machines that seemed to echo in the dimly lit room. Of course, the machine next to my bed, keeping rhythm with my breathing, seemed to be the loudest. I wondered how long I would have to be attached to it. Perhaps tomorrow or the next day the tube in my mouth running down my throat to my lungs would be removed and I would be able to talk. Then the thought came flooding into my mind: *Will I ever breathe on my own again? If not, surely I will die. How does one live without being able to breathe? How does one live and not speak? Will I want to live if I can't talk or teach?*

Later the next afternoon, I learned the awful truth. I was going to surgery to have a tracheotomy so I could breathe from a machine for the rest of my life. I remember thinking, *That surgery is a little different from having your appendix or gall bladder removed.* The expression "pull the plug" took on new meaning for me.

Although the implantation of the cuffed tracheotomy tube made breathing much more comfortable, the system had its drawbacks. Neither on inspiration or expiration did it allow the airflow to pass through the vocal cords— thus preventing any vocalization. As needs arose, I tried to mouth words and was grateful when family and friends could understand what I was saying. Before long, my children came up with different eye signals for me to use. Then Ron Wilson, a commercial artist and good friend of ours, devised a series of charts, and using my eye signals I was able to communicate even more.

Because of Ron's chart, I was able to let Jo Anne know that I did not want to be left alone during the night. There were always people during the day, but at night I would become very anxious. A group of men from our church worked out a schedule so that someone would always be with me at night. These wonderful men would sit by my side through the long hours of the night and read to me when I was unable to sleep. One man, sensing my uneasiness in the early morning hours, had a beautiful voice and would softly sing familiar hymns that I loved so much.

As the days passed, I was not given any hope that I would ever speak again. I wondered if I would be able to deal with this on a long-term basis. How could I possibly live under these circumstances? Although I could not vocally pray as I usually did, my silent prayers were heard. Even though I did not know if I would ever walk or breathe again and lead a normal life, I knew that somehow, ultimately, everything would be okay. I had resigned myself to the fact that the vent and I were like Siamese twins, joined at the hip—or at the throat, I should say. I would never go anywhere without it for the rest of my life.

After two weeks, I was transferred to a rehabilitation hospital. As my health improved, about six weeks after my arrival, they traded out my cuffed trach for a cuffless trach, which allowed the air to pass by my vocal cords. I was finally able to talk and announced, "My name is Jack. I broke my back." As grateful as I was to use my voice again, it wasn't a normal speech pattern. There would always be a long pause mid-sentence. It made for bad joke telling because I always had to wait for the next breath to come before I could finish what I was saying. Teaching and public speaking seemed to be a thing of the past.

As I grew accustomed to speaking on a vent, the speech therapist introduced me to the Passy-Muir Speaking Valve. To me it was a miracle. It had been invented only five years before I got hurt by David Muir, a creative young man with muscular dystrophy who was frustrated at not being able to speak normally. This little valve (placed just inside the flex tube attached to my neck) forced the air on its way out past the vocal cords and up through the mouth and nasal cavities. In a sense, my head became a wind tunnel. However, I could now speak on the inhale and exhale. "Jack is back," I said with great hope. Little did I comprehend at the time that the way was being paved for me to lead a functional and productive life while living on a ventilator.

Another piece of technology that we found useful was introduced to us by our good friend, Ken Rogers. He perceived how dangerous it was for Jo Anne to leave me alone in the van while running into a store, even for just a few minutes. Ken, an electrical engineer, thought about the problem for a day or two and then came to our home with some small handheld

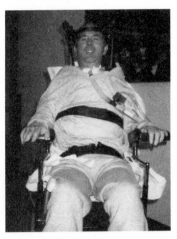

Jack at Rancho Los Amigos
Rehabilitation Hospital.

radios that transmitted an astonishing distance. We used these for some time but have now replaced them with cell phones and Bluetooth technology. Now Jo Anne can leave me in the van with confidence for a few minutes while she takes care of business in her favorite stores. It is comforting to me to say, "Jo Anne, where are you?" More often than not she replies, "I'm at the return desk!" I ask, "How long will you be there?" She responds, "Just a couple of minutes." Translation: probably twenty or thirty minutes. We are even getting the hang of radio talk, which we still use with our cell phones. I usually say "ten four." (I have heard radio people use that phrase; I'm not sure what it means, but it sounds very authoritative and knowledgeable). Jo Anne responds with "seven eleven," which to me makes more sense than "ten four." When I am finished talking, I always say, "Roger, over and out!" I don't know what that means either, but I like Jo Anne's response better than mine as she counters with "In-N-Out."

When people who are dependent on a ventilator are unable to speak and are having trouble breathing, they make a clicking noise with their tongue, which is the universal call for help. The hope is that someone will hear and understand and come to the rescue. One afternoon while I was working on the computer in my office, my hose dislodged from my throat and landed on my chest. The machine mistook it as still working, and the alarm did not go off. I began clicking my tongue with all my might. Jo Anne and the girls were cooking in the kitchen and did not hear me. However, our little dog, Poco, who looked like the dog on the Taco Bell commercials, came running into my office. He sensed my danger, ran into the kitchen, and barked until Jo Anne came and saved my life. Ever since that day, Taco Bell has been my favorite eating establishment.

Sometimes in the midst of a heated conversation, Jo Anne has been known to pull my air hose off my neck just as I am about to make an important point. End of conversation . . . end of life? Breathing and speaking are the best!

Dad/Grandpa/Jack

A Breathtaking
NECKTIE

I LOVE THE Christmas season for many reasons. One thing I enjoy is going to church and seeing the astonishing array of holiday neckties worn by the men and boys. I have always been intrigued by neckties—who invented them, why we wear them, and their purpose. I used to have quite a collection that I enjoyed wearing, but many years ago I traded them all in for just one "breathtaking necktie" that became a permanent part of my attire following my body surfing accident.

This breathtaking necktie connects me to my mechanical ventilator, which pumps twelve breaths of air into my lungs per minute. I love every one of them. I would not be here without this necktie that connects me to my life support system.

Since my accident, my life support has failed me several times. All but one of those times, Jo Anne has been able to bring me back from a state of unconsciousness without involving the medical world. By squeezing the trusty ambubag (a hand-operated air pump), she pumps life-saving oxygen into my lungs. She does this over and over again until I come back from the dead (so it seems), and then reconnects me to the ventilator.

The one time Jo Anne could not revive me, I was in a coma for eight hours and required the assistance of police, paramedics, and hard-working ER/ICU professionals. All of this was accompanied by much prayer. I have no recollection of what happened before I went into the coma. When I finally awoke in the hospital, the last thing I could recall doing was eating a hot dog at Costco. Was it the Costco hot dog that almost did me in? Although I don't seem to enjoy them nearly as much as I used to, Costco will be relieved to know it wasn't a tainted hot dog that nearly killed me but a malfunction of my life support system.

It is a humbling experience to absolutely know—not in theory, but in actual fact—that if I am disconnected from my life support, death will quickly follow within a few short minutes. I am not a medical doctor and have not researched the subject, but I would imagine that most people die because they quit breathing.

Let me share with you another episode that I remember vividly. One evening, a few years ago, Jo Anne and I went out to dinner with our friends. The food there is usually pretty good, but that night my taquitos were buried in some kind of red sauce, which made them soggy and mushy. I had a hard time getting them down. It wasn't my favorite meal, but the company was enjoyable and salvaged the evening.

Dinner with friends.

When we got home, Jo Anne set me up with the TV in my bedroom to watch the Dodgers/Arizona Diamondbacks baseball game, which was in about the sixth inning. The score was tied at two runs each, and a warm feeling began to swell within me that perhaps this evening the Dodgers would not snatch defeat from the jaws of victory as they so typically do. I had watched but a short time when the Arizona Diamondbacks began to hit everything the Dodger pitchers were "throwing up" to the plate. Before I knew it, the score was five to two in favor of the Diamondbacks, with two men on base. At that moment I heard a very loud screeching noise, like a high-pitched siren, and my ventilator went completely dead.

In the many years I had been on a ventilator, I had never heard that noise before, nor had my ventilator ever quit working without any warning. Of course I panicked when I realized I wasn't breathing, but I tried to be positive and told myself that Jo Anne would rush into the room any second, discover the problem, and get me breathing once again. I waited but she didn't come . . . and she didn't come . . . and she didn't come! I finally entered a state of resignation, knowing that she was not coming and that I would soon be dead.

The sad thing about the entire experience is that as I began to enter the twilight zone—half alive and half dead—I was still watching the baseball game. Just as I was slipping into unconsciousness, an Arizona Diamondback hit a three-run home run over the deepest part of centerfield off of Joe Biemel, a journeyman left-handed relief pitcher that nobody but the Dodgers wanted. In the foggy recesses of my mind came the voice of Vince Scully: "And now the score is eight to two in favor of the Diamondbacks." *What a way to go into the spirit world*, I thought—a bad Mexican dinner in my stomach and the Dodgers being hammered by the hated Diamondbacks.

The next thing I remember, Jo Anne was standing over me, weeping and hollering at me while trying to get me to come back. All I knew was that I needed more air and was saying as loud as I could, "Bag me! Bag me!" Awakening out of my catatonic state, I did not realize she was doing just that with the ambubag while trying to dial 911 at the same time. The more she bagged, the more the life came back to me, and she was soon able to move my wheelchair over to the bedside where she hooked me up to my backup ventilator that I use at night. I have no idea how long I was out, but I easily could have slipped into the spirit world, and it would not have been a painful experience except for the memory of the bad Mexican dinner and the Dodgers/Diamondbacks game.

I know of nothing more humbling than not being able to breathe. When you can't breathe, nothing else matters at all!

Recently I was visiting a good friend of mine who has been in the hospital and on life support for a few months due to an accident. As we were visiting, his respiratory therapist came in the room and saw me. He was amazed when he learned I had been ventilator dependent for twenty years. He told me that for many years he had worked with a number of young men on life support and that most of them had not lived more than a couple of years. He was astonished at my quality of life. Talking to this respirator therapist and seeing his reaction to me made me realize how fortunate I am to still be here.

I have often referred to my situation as "living on the edge." Each time I have a brush with death, I consider it another incredible wake-up call. With every encounter, I have reinforced into my mind and heart how precious the gift of life is and how quickly it can be taken from us. I find renewed motivation to live each day as though it were my last. I also notice that Jo Anne treats me a little better—at least for a while.

At times I have been tempted to vegetate and take it easy. After all, who could blame a poor paralyzed man on life support for doing that? Thankfully, I have realized that coasting requires little effort and usually is done downhill. I have come to understand that dying is easy—it is the living that is hard and demanding. Feelings of gratitude have welled up in my heart for the love I have felt from God, my family, and my friends. My loved ones have said things to me that are usually reserved for one's funeral service. I am grateful to have heard them while still alive, because I believe it is better to be seen and spoken to than to be "viewed" and talked about.

My rather unique situation has helped me understand and appreciate the truthfulness of what Jesus taught his apostles just before going into the Garden of Gethsemane: "I am the true vine. . . . Abide in me, and I in you. As the branch cannot bear fruit of itself, except it abide in the vine; no more can ye, except ye abide in me. . . . I am the vine, ye are the branches: He that abideth in me, and I in him, the same bringeth forth much fruit: *for without me ye can do nothing*" (John 15:1–5; emphasis added).

John accurately recorded what the Lord said to the apostles on that occasion. Jesus didn't just say he was "the vine," but that he was "the *true* vine." That statement implies that we can attach ourselves to other vines—false philosophies, precepts, organizations, and so on. But unless we attach ourselves to the true vine, we will not be able to bring forth "much fruit." As the Savior said, "The branch cannot bear fruit of itself, except it abide in the vine." Unless we are attached to our spiritual life support—Christ—*we can do nothing!*"

I am convinced that we are each as dependent on Christ each minute and hour of the day for our spiritual life support as I am dependent on my electrical and mechanical life support system. I know with a sure knowledge that if I attach myself to the "true vine," I will find peace and indescribable joy.

Dad / Grandpa / Jack

March
MADNESS

I HAVE BEEN an avid follower of March Madness—the men's basketball NCAA tournament—for many years. I hate to admit it, but I am a basketball junkie. Even at my age and in my physical condition, there is still a fire burning inside me for this sport. My love for basketball is irrefutable evidence of a misspent youth playing basketball anywhere and everywhere I could, and as often as I could.

From the time I was a very young boy, I loved to play basketball. We had an alley that ran along the side of our house in Ruth, Nevada. My dad and older brothers sunk a large post in a hole they dug in that alley next to our back fence, nailed a makeshift backboard to the post approximately ten feet high, and screwed a rim onto the backboard. This would be our basketball court for years to come. We played basketball all year long. In winter we would shovel the snow away from the basket as best we could and then with heavy coats, mittens, wool stocking caps, and overshoes we would play basketball for hours at a time. As spring gradually arrived, and the dirt in the alley began to thaw, we would play in the mud, And as spring turned into summer, we would play in the dust. I tried to practice the piano and clarinet before school so that it would not interfere with my basketball after school. I would run into the house, throw my books onto the table, grab the basketball, and head for the alley. I didn't care if there was nobody to play with. If I was alone, I would shoot hundreds of jump shots, pretending I was shooting the winning basket for the White Pine County High School Bobcats."

I humbly admit that because of all the practice I became a deadly three-point shooter. The only trouble was that in my era, you only got two points for a basket, regardless of the distance. One of my fantasies was to play on the varsity high school basketball team. As a young boy, I attended every high school basketball game possible. My heart would almost leap out of my chest as the Bobcats came running out onto the floor dressed in their magnificent blue warm-ups and the band played while the crowd sang, "On Ye Bobcats, On Ye Bobcats.

During my junior year in high school, twelve boys made the varsity basketball team. I was number twelve. My joy was complete the night of our first game as I ran out onto the court in my glorious blue warm-ups and the band and crowd sang our fight song.

Up until the time I was hurt, I played basketball with coworkers, on church teams and with my kids, neighbors, and relatives at family gatherings. One afternoon I was playing basketball with some of my students. I dove for a loose ball at the same time one of my students grabbed it and swung his body around. I drove my two front teeth into his shoulder, and one of them snapped off. There was blood everywhere, and he had to have twelve stitches in his shoulder. We kept playing for about another hour, however, which reveals much about my mentality.

When I finally went home, I walked up behind Jo Anne, put my hands over her eyes, and said, "When you look at me don't be too upset. I'm sure it can be fixed." She turned around, and I smiled at her. She screamed. I guess I looked like the village idiot, and though I wanted it, I didn't get much sympathy from my wife. She didn't think a basketball game was quite as important as a tooth.

Jo Anne, who could not understand my passion for this sport in the early years of our marriage, is now as grateful as I am for the entertainment it has provided me following my injury. Since my paralysis, it has brought me hours of enjoyment that otherwise might have been filled with self-pity and boredom. While watching a game, I actually lose my sense of self and become fully involved in what I am watching. For a short time, my body becomes irrelevant, and there is no distinction between me and the other fans who are also caught up in the moment.

One year March Madness almost cost me my life. Jo Anne and I had taken our youngest daughter, Jackie, to St. George, Utah, to visit some of Jo Anne's family. It was toward the end of March, and I was a little nervous that I would not be able to see the NCAA championship game. My whole trip brightened considerably when Jo Anne's brother, Danny, who lives in Mesquite, Nevada, invited me to his home to watch the championship game on his big-screen TV.

I eagerly accepted his invitation. But wouldn't you know, the day before the great event, the battery to my ventilator on the back of my wheelchair died. Jo Anne tried to locate a new one but could not find the right battery in all of St. George. The medical supply store found a garage that said they could order one, but it might take a few days to get it.

The ventilator worked just fine as long as it was plugged into an outlet in the wall. I figured that since breathing is better than not breathing, I had no choice but to stay put. Not much fun for a vacation. Then a light went on in my head—pure revelation. My ventilator is equipped with an internal battery. It is a safety feature in case the main battery dies and I'm not near an outlet. If fully charged, it is supposed to last about one hour—something we hadn't yet put to the test. I knew that it was less than an hour's drive from St. George to Mesquite, and the way Jo Anne drives, it would be even shorter.

I finally convinced Jo Anne to take me and promised her that it would be okay. Late in the afternoon on the day of the game, she and Jackie loaded me into the van and off we went. However, I did not calculate in my plan the unexpected.

Just as we were about to get on the freeway, Jo Anne realized we needed gas. As if that weren't enough, we took the wrong off-ramp to get to Danny's home and got lost. We were still some distance from our destination when the internal battery ran out of juice. At that moment we discovered that when the ventilator dies, it gives a big, sickening gasp—its last breath and mine—and completely shuts down. The next sound is another safety feature. An alarm begins ringing. It is quite a gut-wrenching sound to the person depending on the ventilator.

Because Jo Anne would be at the wheel, we had prepared Jackie, who was not yet twelve (we train them young at our house), for the worst case scenario. Ready and able to help her dad, she pulled out the trusty ambubag and began pumping air into my lungs via my trach attached to my neck. As she pumped, Jackie realized she had me in a very compromising situation that she could use to her advantage.

While pumping like a good daughter, she started asking questions. "Dad, can I have a new bicycle?"

"Yes," I gasped. "Yes, anything, just keep pumping!"

"Dad, how about a year's pass to Disneyland?"

"Yes," I agreed again. "Just keep squeezing that bag!"

We finally screeched to a stop in front of Danny's house, and he came running out to the driveway with a long extension cord. The ventilator was happy once again as it took over the job of pumping air into my lungs to the relief of us all, especially Jackie, who had done such a good job. In fact, she had an incredible smile on her face. I could just picture visions of bicycles and Disneyland dancing in her head.

Plugged into the wall, munching on chips and dip, drinking root beer, and watching Arizona beat Kansas on the big-screen TV, I was truly in heaven. I temporarily put out of my mind the fact that later that night—it turned out to be midnight—we would have to make the mad dash back up the gorge to St. George to the safety of another extension cord and wall socket. Jo Anne, giving a great imitation of an Indy 500 driver, got us home early.

Am I crazy, or what? Was it really worth risking my life to watch that game on the big-screen TV? Any normal, rational person would say, "Of course not!" But for somebody infected with the March Madness disease, it was worth the risk.

I hope those of you with sound minds will have mercy on those of us who are smitten by March Madness. If you unfortunately happen to be married to someone with this affliction, let me give you the following counsel: As you offer your prayers for your loved one, pattern your words after those of the distraught father who brought his son to Jesus to be healed. "Lord, have mercy on my son [husband]: for he is [a] *lunatic*" (Matthew 17:15; emphasis added). And we must never forget Paul's counsel to the Thessalonian Saints: "Comfort the feebleminded" (1 Thessalonians 5:14).

On the bright side, March comes only once every twelve months!

Dad/Grandpa/Jack

OBSERVATION FIVE

SIP 'N' PUFF

THANKFULLY, I HAVE some mobility because of my breath control wheelchair. Christopher Reeve—Superman—had one exactly like mine. Some call it a "sip 'n' puff wheelchair" since that is how it is controlled. Because I have zero movement in my head or neck, my only alternative is this type of chair.

Living in a wheelchair presents some interesting challenges. I initially felt very self-conscious whenever I would go out in public. For instance, when I go outside I like to wear a ball cap, but Jo Anne will hardly ever let me because she says it makes me look too conspicuous.

The perceptions of little children regarding me in a wheelchair are very interesting. Their comments are always right on target. My four-year-old nephew who had not seen me since my accident was mesmerized by my condition. He wanted to know why I couldn't walk, so I gave him an in-depth explanation about how my spinal cord had been severed. Just as I was concluding my discourse, he impatiently asked, "Well, can you crawl?" His baby sister was doing just that on the floor nearby, and he yelled at her, "You better get out of the way or he will squash you!"

Awhile back we were meeting some of our children and grandchildren at a Mexican restaurant. When our daughter informed our three-year-old granddaughter that they were meeting us to eat tacos, she said, "Grandpa can't eat tacos—his hands are stuck. Even his feet are stuck. Why, his whole body is stuck in that wheelchair!"

I'll never forget the time I went to see my little daughter in a school program. As we were leaving, we crossed paths with a group of five-year-olds having recess. As they gathered around me, they started bombarding me with questions. I was rather shocked when one little boy got really close to me, looked up into my eyes, and said, "Hey mister, what happened to your face?" "My face?" I hollered. Why, I thought my face was the only part of me that halfway worked! I wanted to run over the kid.

Some time ago I received my third new chair since my accident. Each chair has been much better than the previous model. I have adapted to my new chair very quickly, thankfully. A wheelchair for somebody in my condition really becomes an extension of his body.

I control my chair by giving commands through sipping and puffing on a hard plastic straw that I hold between

Granddaughter Sabrina Riley goes for a ride.

my teeth, which activates micro switches that control all the functions of the chair. I also have a small display by my left hand that enables me to see in which mode the chair is operating. I have four different drive modes that have been programmed by a computer to meet my specific needs and desires. My first drive mode I call "the church drive," which I designed to be very gentle, especially as I turn. Drive 2 is my "all-purpose drive." I had it programmed to go faster than drive 1 in all directions, yet it is safe enough to use at church or at home. Drive 3 I call "ramming speed." It is strictly an outdoor mode in which I can flat-out move. I use it driving to the park, for example, or in Costco. There is enough kid still in me to enjoy letting it go full blast and then seeing how tightly I can turn my chair. All of you without wheelchairs are really missing out on a lot of fun. Drive

4 is "the attendant control drive." Jo Anne operates it, so I had it programmed to be gentler than the church drive as a life preserving and precautionary measure.

The chair is a new concept created by Invacare Corporation. They won many engineering awards for its design. It has six wheels—two small ones in front and in back and then two larger wheels at the right and left center of the chair. It is called a center-wheel drive. It has great stability, and the back two wheels even have shocks to make the ride more comfortable. My particular model allows me to also tilt and recline, which comes in handy during some church meetings. The make of my wheelchair is Storm TDX 3. That name alone is enough to get my blood pumping. The only problem I have with the wheelchair is that it is much smarter than I am.

Although each new chair is better and safer than the previous one, if I am not careful, I can still run into things, over things, and off of stairs and curbs. I always have to remember to be alert and careful, take nothing for granted, and not get lulled into a sense of false security while driving about. I am just an accident waiting to happen.

My first chair seemed to have a lot of safety issues. If I hit a bump in the road or sidewalk, it would disconnect the sip and puff mechanism, preventing me from controlling the chair. It would be like driving a car at fifty miles an hour without being able to steer it or apply the brakes. It was very frightening!

On one occasion, Jo Anne and I went to Sea World in San Diego to attend a social with some of our colleagues. As I drove in my chair from the parking lot to the restaurant, I had to maneuver my way over some rough cobblestone lanes. When we arrived at the entrance to the restaurant, Jo Anne, walking in front of me, entered the main area. I was unable to follow her because, at that very moment, I realized that the sip and puff connection had become disconnected. Unable to change modes, I started rolling down a long hallway at the end of which was a long flight of stairs. I just knew I was going to roll down them and end my mortal life. I hate to admit it, but I panicked and instead of screaming "Help," I started screaming "Jo Anne, Jo Anne!" Just before I reached the stairs, a good friend of mine came up out of the stairwell, grabbed my wheelchair, and pushed it into the wall, where it continued to grind away. Others heard my cries for Jo Anne, and she soon appeared on the scene and turned off the chair. It was, to say the least, a very harrowing experience.

I enjoy driving around our neighborhood in my wheelchair. One evening, Jo Anne and I were out rolling—me in my first generation chair and she on her bicycle. I went over a bump in the road, and it caused me to lose control of the chair as I had at Sea World. I hollered at Jo Anne, but before she could get to me and hit the "kill switch" (which is designed to stop the chair immediately—isn't that a nice name for someone in my predicament), the chair turned up a driveway and crashed into the back of a new Thunderbird. This not only stopped the chair, but the impact also caused the chair to wedge into the bumper in such a way that neither Jo Anne or I could get it loose. She was forced to knock on the owner's door to ask for help. A large man opened it, and Jo Anne said, "My husband just ran into your new Thunderbird!" He growled and ran out of the house. He was speechless when he saw my wheelchair stuck to the back of his beautiful red Thunderbird. Finally, he took action and was able to dislodge my chair. Fortunately, the damage was minimal for both of us, and he seemed happy to just see us continue on our way.

Another potential disaster was the day I was tooling down the hallway in our church. Without warning, a door suddenly opened in front of me, and a huge seeing-eye dog with his blind master entered the hallway. Upon seeing me rolling toward his master at top speed, the dog went ballistic trying to save him from impending danger. The blind man, in shock and total confusion, wanted to know what was happening. Fortunately, I stopped before running over the dog and knocking this good man down. Jo Anne quickly explained the situation and assured him that all was well. I can't recall Jo Anne saying anything comforting or kind to me—I wonder why. Thankfully, no harm was done and we didn't get sued. I could just see the headlines: "Paralyzed man in wheelchair driving at a reckless speed runs over blind man."

I'm grateful there are still technicians who know how to fix the chair. I hope I don't outlive them all. How blessed I am that there are talented people in the world who are trained and have the desire to invent wonderful creations that bless and improve the quality of others' lives.

I probably shouldn't write what I'm going to write next. I'm sure Jo Anne will submit my name and some of my escapades to the following website I recently found called "The Darwin Awards." According to the home page, it is "a chronicle of enterprising demises or near demises honoring those who improve the species . . . by accidentally removing themselves from it!"

For example, one incident that almost received the top Darwin award a few years ago is as follows: Two young men living in Wisconsin went ice fishing for the first time. It was bitter cold, and they were ill prepared for this event. They had all their gear in the back of a beautiful brand-new red truck, along with their faithful dog. Although they had a special saw to make a hole in the ice, they thought it would take too long, so they got the brilliant idea of blowing a hole in the ice with a stick of dynamite. One of the young men lit the stick of dynamite and threw it as far as he could. The dog, thinking it was a fun game, ran after it. He retrieved it and started running back toward the truck as fast as he could. They tried to wave the dog off, but the more they waved and shouted, the faster he came toward them. Just as he got to the truck, he slipped, slid under the truck, and the dynamite exploded. The only

Rolling through the neighborhood with daughters Rachel and Jackie (ages nine and four).

happy thing about this story, I'm afraid to report, is that the two young men were able to save themselves. I wish I could say the same about the truck and the dog.

I believe that all of us have probably done something to qualify for a Darwin award sometime during our lives. Just as I have to be constantly alert when driving my wheelchair so I don't injure myself or someone else, we all must be alert on our spiritual path. When we become careless in our spiritual drive through life, we can lose control and get off the narrow path. In the process, we can destroy ourselves and possibly our loved ones as well. We need to be careful never to be candidates for a spiritual Darwin award.

Dad/Grandpa/Jack

Living on the
EDGE

WHEN I WAS nineteen years old, I worked for Kennecott Copper Corporation in Ruth, Nevada, and drove a huge earth-moving truck called a Uke. The trucks were monstrous. We had to climb up a short ladder to get into the cab, which always seemed to me like sitting on the roof of our house because we were so high above the road. These trucks had tires that were taller than I was and an automatic transmission, so all I had to do was put it in reverse or drive and push on the gas pedal.

In the beginning, driving this truck was scary because most of it was done at night. But after several weeks, I became confident in my ability to drive the truck and truly felt that I was invincible. One cool October morning, I was hauling a large load of ore from the bottom of the pit to the top. My mind was wandering, and I wasn't thinking of the tons of truck and ore that I was hauling. Because of my day-dreaming, I drove too close to the edge of the road and hit a soft shoulder. Like a huge elephant, the truck began to tip over on its side. Thankfully, I was not on the side of the road that would put me in danger of tipping over into the mile-deep pit. I was going so slowly that the track just settled over onto its side and the engine kept running. The passenger side went down into the dirt, and I hung onto the steering wheel with all my might.

The truck didn't have a seat belt, and I was safe from injury only because I didn't let go of the wheel. I quickly stood up and tried to reach the handle on the opposite door, but the cab was so big that I couldn't reach the handle to get out of the truck. Some men who were working nearby heard the noise, saw what happened, and came running to help me. They were able to get the door open and dragged me out. I was in a state of shock as I realized how badly I could have been hurt. My boss drove up and chastised me with language I had never heard before.

From that time on, I was very conscientious and became a good truck driver. I learned through that experience how fragile life can be. Little did I know then that I would have a similar experience later in my life.

Our youngest daughter, Jackie, once said to her mother, "If Dad were 'normal' like everyone else, life would be so boring!" I proved her point by bringing a little excitement back into our lives after a relatively quiet period. Our three married daughters, a daughter-in-law, and eight of our grandchildren came to our home, and Jo Anne and I went with them to a nice park for a picnic. We had Subway

Overlooking Bryce Canyon in Utah.

sandwiches, cookies, chips, and root beer. Life just doesn't get much better than that!

The sun was shining brightly, but it was cool and I was wearing a black poncho. As long as I faced the sun, I was warm and happy, much like a toad sitting on a hot rock out in the desert.

Facing the way I was, however, I couldn't see the kids playing on the playground equipment, so I decided to reposition myself, even though it meant turning my face away from my friend Mr. Sun.

My eyesight isn't very good, and as I turned toward the playground, I didn't see a barrier between the sidewalk I was on and the playground. But to my utter disbelief there was, and I rolled off it at such an angle into the sand that my wheelchair tipped over on its left side—of course with me in it. I must have resembled a pregnant elephant lying on her side.

Two of my daughters saw me literally "bite the sand," and their screams could have raised the dead. Jo Anne, high on a platform with her young granddaughter, turned toward the screams, fearing what she might see. From her vantage point, she could only see a big black blob lying in the sand, and then, in shock and horror, was able to make out my features and realized the black blob was me.

When my face finally settled into the sand and I realized I was still breathing, my panic quickly disappeared. I have always said, "If you can just breathe, everything else in life is pretty much just icing on the cake."

There I was, over 400 pounds of dead weight (the chair weighing in at least 250—you figure the rest) laying on my side in the sand. Jo Anne, always practical, felt there was no way they could get me up, so she dialed 911. My daughters, my daughter-in-law, some of the bigger grandkids, and several moms who were at the park with their kids tried to push me and the chair upright. Their first effort was unsuccessful, but the second effort—spurred on by massive doses of adrenaline now pumping through their bodies—was successful. I was truly amazed that these women and children were able to get that chair, with me still in it, out of the sand and back on the sidewalk. Whoever said women are the weaker sex should have been at the park that day to realize how false that statement really is.

And so I made my contribution to the picnic by turning it into a very exciting and memorable event. Who said I wasn't good for anything? I must admit, I was a bit offended that Jo Anne called me a black blob, but it was an apt description.

I can't tell you how many times I have driven up to the edge of a drop-off in my wheelchair only to be miraculously stopped before tipping off onto my face. Because of my compromised vision, I agreed with Jo Anne to stay as far away from the edge of the sidewalk as I can and to never proceed in unfamiliar terrain without somebody walking in front of me to show me the way.

Because we have our agency, we can choose to live our lives on the edge of physical or spiritual disaster. One false move sends us over the edge, and we must suffer the consequences of our actions. How wise it is to stay away from the edge of physical or spiritual disaster and follow those who know the safe way.

And what if we do plunge off the edge? Is all lost? I don't think so! King David teetered on the edge of spiritual disaster and then plunged off into an abyss of misery. However, even his disaster taught him a great lesson about the love of the Savior. David wrote: "I waited patiently for the Lord; and he inclined unto me, and heard my cry. He brought me up also out of an horrible pit, out of the miry clay, and set my feet on a rock and . . . has put a new song in my mouth" (Psalm 40:1–3).

Dad/Grandpa/Jack

Mecca of
MERCHANDISE

THE OTHER DAY, Jo Anne asked me if I would like to run some errands with her. She had to return a few things to Walmart and said she would buy me lunch at Taco Bell. The temptation of lunch at Taco Bell was too great for me, and so, against my better judgment, I consented to go with her. Thankfully, and mercifully as it turned out, we went to Taco Bell first, and a bean burrito with extra onions fortified me for the coming ordeal.

We ran several errands after lunch, and then pulled into the parking lot at Walmart. Before that visit, I had only been in one Walmart for just a few minutes. The memory of that visit had somehow retreated into the dark recesses of my mind, so this felt like a new experience.

I was absolutely amazed at the size of the Walmart building. As we entered the front door and I was able to get some perspective on the considerable square footage sheltering innumerable displays and shelves bulging with everything imaginable, I thought, "This must be the mecca of merchandise."

We went to the return counter first, which is standard operating procedure when shopping with Jo Anne. Sadly, the women's section was near the return counter, and Jo Anne turned and began to walk in that direction. The closer we got to that jungle of femininity, the more her pace quickened. Not even my power wheelchair could keep up with her.

Jo Anne had an unnatural gleam in her eye as she disappeared from my view. I found her and stuck with her for a minute or two. But as she filled her shopping cart with garments she would have to try on, a feeling of despair began to get the best of me. She suggested I park my wheelchair by the women's dressing room and wait for her there. I was obedient, but I had only been there a short time when several employees asked if they could help me and wondered if I was waiting for someone. I suspect they thought I was a little strange staring at the women's dressing room. Fortunately, Jo Anne whizzed by and muttered under her breath that maybe I should roll around a bit because she would be a few more minutes.

Based on past experience, I took her invitation to heart and began my exploration of Walmart. I picked a wide aisle and motored down it to the home entertainment section. There I discovered row after row of DVDs of possibly every

Shopping with Jo Anne.

movie ever made. I read many of the titles and felt that I hadn't missed too much by not seeing most of them. I neared the music section but was blasted away by a fellow shopper who was testing a state-of-the-art sound system. Again, a friendly Walmart employee asked if he could help me. I said no, but we chatted for a minute or two.

Then I wheeled into the automotive department, where I was overcome by all the automotive accoutrements. I must admit I started salivating as I discovered all the things I could buy for our van. Again, a friendly employee (they seemed to be everywhere) asked if he could help me, and another visit ensued. I now knew several employees by their first names—what a friendly bunch.

To the right of the automotive department was my favorite section, the sports department. I spent a lot of time in that section, amazed at everything that was available for every kind of sport. I enjoyed a pleasant conversation with another employee, who was probably wondering who had let me out on the loose. Afterward, I quickly bypassed the gardening, kitchenware, and bedding and bathroom aisles. But I slowed down at the men's department and soon found myself back in front of the women's dressing room.

By then, I figured we had been in Walmart nearly three hours. As Jo Anne dashed out of the dressing room and back to the racks, I noticed her pace had slackened a bit. I took courage and faith that exhaustion would soon get the best of her and we could leave the "mecca of merchandise." But, to her credit, she had more stamina than I thought possible, and it was another hour before we left with her treasures.

Realizing she had probably pushed my patience to the outer limits, Jo Anne volunteered to take me to In-N-Out Burger on the way home. Isn't *home* a wonderful word? Jo Anne is very savvy, and with a cheeseburger, fries, and a root beer under my belt, I returned to my normal, pleasant self.

Is there a moral to this story? I thought about sharing one with Jo Anne but feared if I did, I would never see a Taco Bell or In-N-Out Burger again. Can you think of a better one that would keep me out of trouble?

Dad / Grandpa / Jack

Hit the Ball and
DRAG JACK

AS YOU CAN imagine, my injury has significantly changed my relationship with Jo Anne. I like to compare our new relationship to two golfers. Early one morning, Jack's friend took him golfing. It began to get late, and his wife grew worried about her husband and Jack. Finally, she heard his car coming into the driveway and ran out to meet him. He was disheveled and looked exhausted. His wife wanted to know why he had been gone so long, and he said, "Well, on the first hole, Jack had a heart attack and all day long it was hit the ball and drag Jack!"

That pretty much illustrates our lifestyle and marriage relationship. Jo Anne hits the ball and drags me around.

Awhile back I foolishly let Jo Anne talk me into buying a new modified van. We aren't rich—just stupid, I suppose. Not knowing my life expectancy, I told her I would like to go out in style when it was my time. She thought this was a good idea. I must admit, I was a tad disappointed she agreed so readily to any plan I had regarding my demise.

In our new van, we seem to float effortlessly and silently down the freeway. Driving down the same freeway in our old van was like traveling in a creaking covered wagon with iron rims and no shocks.

Our new van is the fourth one we have purchased since my accident. Thankfully, each one has been a little bit better than the one that preceded it. These are modified minivans with a ramp that automatically lowers itself out of the side of the van when the door is opened. Jo Anne then backs up my wheelchair into the van and locks it into place next to the driver's seat.

The first three vans had a suspension system that was extremely unreliable. It consisted of airbags that would pop out at the most inopportune times and make driving impossible. We never felt confident we would make it to our destination without having a problem. Once when we were traveling from Las Vegas to Southern California, one of the airbags exploded just outside of Barstow, California. Jo Anne was able to maneuver the van to the nearest off ramp and to a fast food restaurant, which was the first establishment we came to. While our youngest daughter, Jackie, watched over me, Jo Anne began the arduous and frustrating process of trying to get the van repaired. Because of my physical condition and size of my wheelchair, it is impossible for me to be transported about in just any ordinary vehicle, so I'm not

good for much in these kinds of situations. Nobody in Barstow knew how to fix our van, but the company in Arizona that had modified the van finally agreed to pay for us to be taken to Southern California with all of us sitting up high on the back of a tow truck. It was the safest trip we ever took in that van for a number of reasons. One of the biggest was that Jo Anne wasn't driving. Thankfully, our newest van has a wonderful suspension system, and we actually feel we have a good chance to reach our destinations without having a harrowing and dangerous experience.

Awhile back Jo Anne loaded me into our new van, and we drove over to the neighborhood car wash. I always have mixed feelings when we get the van all spruced up. I'm happy that the van is going to look so nice, but there is also a definite downside to the experience. When we get to the giant vacuum cleaners that emit a sound similar to that of a wild and tempestuous tornado, Jo Anne lets the ramp down, guides me carefully to earth, and then the humiliation begins. She begins vacuuming me and my wheelchair with the larger-than-life vacuum hose. I always hope nobody will be around to observe the spectacle, but inevitably a few curious onlookers gather around to see whether I will get sucked up into the giant vacuum tank along with the other dirt and debris. What bothers me the most is that they seem to enjoy watching me suffer, and I even suspect they make bets as to whether Jo Anne will send me through the car wash as well.

One day after I had been thoroughly cleansed by the Moby vacuum cleaner and the van was all shiny and clean, I started driving my chair toward the van, anxious to be welcomed into its safe environs and away from public scrutiny. I was going about as fast as my chair would go, and when I gave it the command to stop, it didn't stop! I was helpless and panicked but could do nothing to save myself. And worst of all, I was about to hit my shiny new van. I collided with the front passenger door full blast and heard a sickening wrenching noise. The right leg rest on my wheelchair was crushed and fell to the ground. Of course my leg was all bruised up, but because I couldn't feel anything, that was the least of my worries. The only thought in my mind was, "What have I done to my van?"

I had just left a big gash on the door that resembled the mark of Zorro. It could have been worse, and I was relieved that it wasn't, but I can't say I was proud to have put the first ding on our new van.

One of our best friends is Tony, the car body repairman. He

always has a big smile on his face when we drive up. I wonder why. I hate to admit it, but we have given him a lot of business over the years. Although I am not bragging, in twenty years the only damage I have done to our vans was at the car wash. All the business we have brought Tony's way has resulted from Jo Anne's unique brand of driving by the braille system.

It is always a great adventure having Jo Anne drag me about in our van. Imagine being paralyzed from the neck down and sitting right next to the driver's seat, unable to cover your eyes with your hands, or protect yourself in any way. Every lane change on the freeway is a heart-stopping experience. It got so bad I had to get a pacemaker to survive our excursions.

Now, I have a lot of patience and am usually quite pleasant to be around, but Jo Anne's driving can at times get the best of me. We were driving along in a peaceful neighborhood one day looking for an address when she made a dangerous maneuver that about cost us our lives. The devil inside got the best of me, and I barked at her. She looked at me with a pained expression on her face and said, "Ronald Reagan would never have talked to Nancy that way." I agreed with her but then added that Nancy probably never drove the way she did.

Once we were late for a speaking engagement. Jo Anne was going at least forty miles per hour as we entered the parking lot and didn't notice the huge speed bump. We hit it hard. I came out of my wheelchair, hit my head on the ceiling, lost both of my shoes, and almost slid out of my wheelchair as I came back down. Two young teenagers were standing there watching the entertainment, and Jo Anne enlisted their help to hoist me back up into the chair.

One afternoon Jo Anne borrowed our youngest son's old Toyota to drive to the local market. The car was banged up with dents everywhere and wasn't pleasant to look at. In the parking lot, Jo Anne made an interesting maneuver and almost hit another car. The driver of the other car rolled his window down and hollered, "Hey lady, no wonder your car looks like that!"

However, being dragged about in our van does add some zest and excitement to my life. I think all of us enjoy taking a ride and having that kind of mobility. Recently, an Amish man wrote me a letter. Somehow, in Pennsylvania, he had read about me and wanted to tell me about his situation. He is the father of nine children, and several years ago he rented a minivan and a driver to take them on a longer trip than feasible with their traditional horse and buggy. An unfortunate accident occurred as they were coming home. His nine-month-old daughter lost her life, and he was injured like me. The Amish community consented for him to put electricity into his home so that he could be on a ventilator. They also permitted him to purchase a computer with voice recognition software, which he uses as a typewriter. He doesn't use the Internet at all. In his letter he described how his buggy had been modified with a plywood ramp that drops out of the back so he can drive his wheelchair up and into that conveyance. In my mind's eye I can see this wonderful Amish quadriplegic on life support being pulled about in his modified horse and buggy.

When you have impaired mobility and can't do anything on your own, what a joy it is to be married to someone like Jo Anne, who is willing to hit the ball and drag Jack.

Dad/Grandpa/Jack

SECTION TWO

CAREGIVING

What Constitutes an
ACCIDENT?

THE OTHER DAY I noticed Jo Anne studying my life insurance policy. She informed me that if I were to suffer an accidental death, she would receive double the face value of the policy. Then (and later this kind of disturbed me a bit), she asked me what could constitute an accidental death for someone in my condition. Without thinking, I blurted out a number of scenarios that would surely do me in and would be viewed by the authorities as accidental death.

I didn't think much about it after that until a week later. It was a Sunday evening, and I had been in bed all day due to a pressure sore on my backside. Jo Anne was leaning over me, adjusting my vent hose, which is attached to my throat on one end and a humidifier on the other end. The hose is about six feet long. The humidifier, which provides necessary moisture to my lungs, is connected by another short hose to the ventilator, which sits on a shelf next to my bed.

Normally the humidifier is permanently attached to the vent, but both had just been replaced, and the new humidifier was too tall when attached to the vent for the shelf above, and so it was left free standing.

Although we had taken precautions to secure the humidifier, Jo Anne accidentally (so she says) tipped it over, and the water immediately went from the humidifier through the long vent hose and into my lungs. I literally started to drown as my lungs filled with water, and I turned purple from lack of oxygen.

Jo Anne was doing everything in her power to help me (which was very comforting given our life insurance policy discussion) and even called 911. After what seemed like forever, several policemen, firefighters, and paramedics arrived at the scene—this wasn't the first time for some of them. These good folks took over for Jo Anne, got some oxygen into me, and rushed me to the ER. Once in the ER, I was stabilized, but thinking I might get bacterial pneumonia, the doctor deemed it wise to keep me in the ICU for a few days for observation and to pump me full of antibiotics.

Jo Anne, feeling guilty I'm sure, spent each night sleeping on her trusty air mattress next to my bed. Needless to say, neither of us got much sleep. Finally, on the third afternoon of my stay, I was released. Jo Anne and our son Richard loaded up the van, and Jo Anne and I headed for home while Rich went back to work. We had gone but a short distance when Jo Anne realized we had forgotten a beautiful vase of flowers our children had given us for our forty-fourth wedding anniversary, which

we had celebrated in the ICU the day before. She turned the van around and fortunately was able to find a parking spot directly in front of the main doors of the hospital. After stopping the van, she made a mad dash to recover the flowers.

While she entered the hospital doors, it seemed like the van was moving backward. Sure enough, in great disbelief and awe, I quickly realized that the van was actually freewheeling backward toward a two-lane road that bordered the hospital. Not knowing if the van would hit another car, or if a car would hit me, the thought occurred to me that this might be my last van ride. If so, this would be the "true accident" that would enable Jo Anne to collect on that accidental death life insurance policy.

The van picked up speed. I guess you would have to be paralyzed from the neck down and unable to turn your head to fully understand my predicament. Finally, the van crossed the two-lane road, missing two large red fire hydrants and an iron rail fence, jumped the curb, ran through a flower bed, and gently stopped as the back bumper came into contact with a newly planted tree. Several nurses and two security guards ran over to investigate the situation. Seeing me in my wheelchair, they quickly ascertained that I had nothing to do with the escapade and were puzzled as to what had happened. I was just as puzzled, and all we could determine was that Jo Anne had put the van in neutral instead of park. I pled with them to go easy on her—no handcuffs—and explained that it was simply an "accident" (I hope!).

As Jo Anne walked out of the hospital, she couldn't see the van and thought that maybe some foolish person had "quadnapped" me. She looked around and was puzzled to see the van in the distance with, what she thought, was a policemen standing next to it. She did not understand why they would repark the van and why they would move it so far away. When she got closer and realized the van was sitting in the middle of a flower bed, they nearly had to get a stretcher for her. She explained her sleepless nights spent with her poor disabled husband in critical care, and they took great pity on her. However, they did point out to her the difference between neutral and park, for which I was grateful.

All the way home she pled her case—"Jack, please believe me. It truly was just an accident!" She was pretty convincing, but she did sound like she was grasping for straws.

Jo Anne is a good sport to let me write about her the way I do. On a more serious note, and one that is very tender to me, she spent all three nights with me in the ICU. Based on my many experiences in the hospital, we know those wonderful nurses simply do not know how to take care of somebody with all of my issues. They don't see many patients like me, for which I am sure they are grateful. I also needed Jo Anne's help because I was on a hospital ventilator that I wasn't used to, and every time I would doze off, an alarm would go off that sounded like a calliope at an amusement park. All through the night whenever Jo Anne would hear the alarm, she would get up and lean over my bed to make sure I was still breathing.

On one occasion when she looked at me, my eyes were wide open with that vacant stare. She thought I had died. She screamed, slapped my face, and started shaking me. I was actually wide awake before the slap, but after that I was very alert! The ICU staff went ballistic, thinking they had a casualty on their hands. I wonder why they were so eager to help us pack and leave the next day. Multiply what Jo Anne did for me in the ICU those three nights by many years of days and nights, and you get a little glimpse of what charity is all about.

This experience was just another bump in the road, and life goes on—

Wait! Did you feel what I just felt? It's either the end of the world or an earthquake! Jo Anne just ran in and said it was an earthquake! Could she have caused it?

Dad / Grandpa / Jack

The House that Jack's
FRIENDS BUILT

A FEW WEEKS ago in our Sunday School class, I taught a lesson about the healing miracles of Jesus, using the Gospel of Mark as our primary source. As usual, the poor members of our class were at my mercy, as I always select the content we will consider. This particular Sunday I chose to spend some time with Jesus' healing of a paralyzed man in Capernaum, Peter and Andrew's hometown. The story is well known and is found in Mark 2:1–12. For some reason, Mark's account of the healing of the paralyzed man is one of my favorite healing incidents recorded in the New Testament. I wonder why.

News spread like wildfire that Jesus was in town. His reputation had preceded Him, and the home He was in was thronged with a multitude of people, making it impossible to even get near the door. The paralyzed man had four friends who took him on a stretcher to the home. They attached ropes to the stretcher and hauled the man up to the rooftop, broke open the roof, and lowered him down at the very feet of Jesus. I like to think that the Savior had a smile on his face as He witnessed the ingenuity and faith these four men displayed in behalf of their paralyzed friend.

Jesus healed the paralyzed man, and in my mind's eye, I can see the five men walking arm in arm down the dusty lane, undoubtedly rejoicing in the great miracle they had just witnessed. They must have talked about this Jesus and who He really was to have the power to perform such a mighty miracle. Perhaps, however, the greatest miracle of all was the miracle of faith, love, kindness, and compassion exhibited by four friends who took the paralyzed man to the feet of Jesus so he could be healed.

My focus on this incident is perhaps a bit different from what many others would stress, which would be the faith of these men and the great healing power of Jesus. To me it is all of that, but it is also so much more. It is a wonderful and inspiring story of love, kindness, compassion, and friendship, involving four unnamed men and their paralyzed friend. I have thought that if Jesus were to come to my "village," my friends, who have faith and ingenuity, would take me to the feet of the Savior so that I could be healed, no matter the cost.

Having received countless acts of kindness and compassion myself during so many years, I can understand how the now healed man must have felt toward his four friends and the Savior.

At the time of my accident, my family was living in a two-story home, and all the bedrooms were upstairs. Jo Anne felt that the only thing we could do under the circumstances was to sell the home and find a single-level plan that would more adequately meet our needs. As she expressed this thought to some friends, they told her that they would never allow us to move. Paul Colby and Gary Anderson, who live in our neighborhood and are members of our church, proposed to Jo Anne that we build an addition onto our home. They were both builders and fine craftsmen and had many friends who also were carpenters and builders. They told Jo Anne that they would build an addition and that the labor and most of the materials would be provided at no cost to us. We were touched by this demonstration of love and concern. A fund-raising project brought in sufficient funds to pay for the materials not donated to complete the addition, as well as a new modified van that I could travel in. This outpouring of love and support from so many people was a miracle to us. We will be grateful to them forever.

In early December 1989, Gary drew up the plans for a 750-square-foot addition that would include a special bedroom to meet my needs, a unique office designed around my wheelchair, and a large dining room that connected the two. Gary quickly submitted the plans for a building permit, as I was scheduled to be released from the hospital at the end of January 1990. That gave the men just six weeks to build the entire addition. They were determined to get the job done so that I could be released on the appointed day.

Gary, anxious to know if the plans had been approved, finally went in person to see what the holdup was. No one was aware of the plans. Gary explained the situation to the man in charge. After locating the plans on the bottom of a large stack of unapproved plans, the man signed the permit on the spot. On a beautiful Saturday morning, men and boys showed up in our backyard and, with picks and shovels, began digging the footings for the foundation of the new addition.

Jo Anne would bring reports to the hospital, including video recordings of the progress of the undertaking. A great spirit of love and unity developed among those who worked so hard and selflessly to complete this addition so that I could go home. The women also worked alongside the men and provided many meals for those who were laboring.

Finally, the day came for my release and homecoming. Jo Anne borrowed an old modified van that I was able to ride in. Unbeknownst to me, everyone who had helped build the addition to our home, as well as many friends from our neighborhood and church, gathered to welcome me home. I knew none of this was taking place and assumed that it would be a quiet event.

Jo Anne had called ahead to let everyone know the approximate time of our arrival. A reporter and photographer from the local newspaper were there to cover the event. As we turned onto our street, I saw that it was lined with friends of all ages holding banners that read, "Welcome Home" and "We Love You." Murl Nelson, a close friend and musician, had his drums set up on the front lawn and was accompanying my mother-in-law, who was singing, "To Dream the Impossible Dream" and "You're Home Again Jack" to the tune of "On the Road Again."

Gary Anderson, Paul Colby, and the other participants in building the addition could hardly wait to show it to me. Gary pushed me around the side of the house where a wide cement walk had been poured to accommodate my wheelchair. To me it looked as big as the Santa Ana Freeway. When I rounded the corner, I was truly amazed at the spectacular addition. The entire back of the house was filled with windows to let in the light. The door to the addition had not yet arrived, so a temporary door was in place. Written on it was, "The House that Jack's Friends Built!" Everyone who had helped had signed their names below those words. I have never been so overwhelmed and touched as I was at that moment. The love that had gone into the building of this beautiful structure was amazing.

It was like a big party as Gary pushed me inside the house to show me each room and all they had done to meet my new needs. Kids were looking through the windows, adults were visiting and walking about, and there was a festive feeling in the air. I was overcome by my feelings of love and gratitude for my family and friends. I will never be able to repay them for what they have done for me. It is largely because of their support that I believe I have been able to deal with my situation in a positive way. I know they will always be greatly blessed for this act of kindness and love.

As time has passed, I have come to appreciate more what my friends did in putting this addition onto the back of our home. Good friends are not easy to come by, and my friends have meant everything to me. Most of my life is spent in these three rooms

From left to right: Jay Dee Barr, Mike Davidson,
Gary Anderson, and Paul Colby.

that my friends built. A day doesn't go by that I am not reminded
of their love and willingness to serve. This addition has such a
beautiful spirit in it—the spirit of love, sacrifice, and pure service.

"And they come unto him, bringing one sick of the palsy,
which was borne of four" (Mark 2:3). Perhaps a worthy goal
in all of our lives would be to be one of the four who made
sure their paralyzed friend was given the opportunity to
come under the healing influence of Christ. No one will
ever know the feelings of joy and gratitude that must have
filled the heart of the formerly paralyzed man.

Dad / Grandpa / Jack

Never Out of
STYLE

YESTERDAY WAS "HAIR" day for me. About every week or week and a half, Jo Anne takes a good, critical look at me and announces that I am unfit to be seen in public. Those words are like a dagger in my heart because I know what is coming and I can't defend myself. She has a little instrument, which runs off batteries, that has tiny blades rotating at a high rpm, and she shoves it up my nose to cut out any extraneous hair. It is only supposed to cut the hair, but inevitably it manages to chew up a little tissue as well. If the rotating blades don't get all the hair, she comes at me with her little scissors—and all the while I am screaming, groaning, and shouting, "Quad abuse!"

With my nose now having achieved a satisfactory rating, she concentrates her efforts on my ears. Accompanied by my groans, screams, and accusatory "quad abuse" statements, she calmly inserts her little scissors in my ears, cuts out any extra hair, and digs out any foreign matter that she doesn't feel should be there. I now give a sigh of relief because the worst is over—but not completely.

Next she attacks my eyebrows and tells me that no husband of hers is ever going to look like Andy Rooney. Then, using a combination electric razor and hair clipper device, she trims my hair—what little I have—to her specified standard of excellence. About this time I am so happy and relieved to have it almost over, but lurking in the back of my mind is the painful thought that this process will be repeated in the not-too-distant future.

By the way, the word *hair* almost cost me my life shortly after my accident. Early one morning in the rehabilitation hospital, a Hispanic nurse's aide—a sweet little woman—was performing a procedure on me. As she worked over me, I could sense that the hose that runs from my throat to the respirator was coming loose and I wasn't breathing very well. I looked at this little lady and gasped, "My air, my air, I'm losing my air!" With great compassion in her eyes and voice she responded, "Mr. Rushton, why are you worried about your hair?" Then with my last breath I murmured, "No, my air, my air." She insightfully rejoined, "You shouldn't worry so much about your hair. It's okay." At that point, the hose popped off my throat, I quit breathing, and the little Hispanic lady never had a clue what was happening. Thankfully the alarms went off, and two nurses ran in from the nursing station to save my life.

Many of my male friends know I regrettably wear "outfits" now since Jo Anne took charge of my wardrobe and started dressing me each morning. I used to have two or three suits, some nice white shirts, a few ties, and some Levis and T-shirts. That pretty much constituted my wardrobe. Life was so simple then, and deciding what to wear each day was not very difficult.

I would be embarrassed if anyone looked in my bedroom closets and saw my many matching outfits. I get dizzy just looking at the dazzling array of finery. But the clothes in my closets are just the tip of the iceberg. Stored in boxes somewhere in the dark recesses of our home reside my summer outfits, fall outfits, and spring outfits. It would be unthinkable for me to wear the same outfit twice in a row or even twice in a two-week period.

My Filipino caregiver, Rey, and I would never dare to choose the outfit for the day. It is totally beyond our capacity to make such a momentous decision. From time to time, Jo Anne goes on a trip without me, and I encourage her to go because she really needs a break. If she is gone fourteen days, she will hang fourteen different outfits from left to right in my closet. Every seventh outfit is a special "Sunday outfit." Would Rey and I ever deviate from the foreordained outfits during her absence? I don't think so! We are both smarter than that and know that somehow Jo Anne would find out.

Please don't think badly of Jo Anne or think she is practicing some form of malicious psychological quad abuse on

Caregiver Rey Duenas gets Jack out of bed.

me. She truly believes the way I look is a reflection of her as my wife and primary caregiver. She doesn't have much quality raw material to work with in me, so she makes a valiant effort to dress me in the best possible outfits on the market. I, of course, can do nothing about this situation, so I make a valiant effort to be pleasant and full of gratitude that I look so handsome. I try my best to keep Jo Anne happy. Can you imagine what she could do to me if I got her angry, which I have inadvertently done on occasion?

I must admit that I feel bad I can't wear a suit and a white shirt and tie to church on Sunday. This is impossible because of my life support system. In spite of Jo Anne's valiant efforts, I feel a little underdressed on Sundays. I have always believed that dressing in my best suit on Sundays is a sign of reverence and respect. I think I developed that feeling from observing my father when I was growing up.

My dad was a miner and later a warehouse employee for Kennecott Copper Corporation. He wore khaki-colored work clothes and boots five or six days a week. However, Sunday was a different matter. He owned only one suit, but it was beautiful, and he purchased it at Goodman-Tidball Mercantile. The only other store in town that sold suits was JCPenney, so Goodman-Tidball was definitely a step up. His white shirt had French cuffs, which he wore with beautiful cuff links. He also had a couple of nice ties and a pair of expensive dress shoes, and he always carefully polished and shined them.

Dad never preached to me about reverence or respect, but demonstrated it to me by his example. Because of him, I wish I could still wear suits, starched white shirts, and beautiful ties to church on Sunday. I do have some nice shoes that are fifteen years old and still look like new. I wonder why.

Even though I tease Jo Anne about my outfits, I am very grateful to be married to somebody who cares so much about how I look. Over the years, I have thought a great deal about the way she dresses and grooms me. I believe she feels others will judge her by the way I look. But more important, I believe she loves me enough to care about things that no one else would even think about. She understands that my groaning and complaining about quad abuse is just a lot of hot air. She knows how much I truly appreciate her desire and willingness to make me feel and look as good as she possibly can.

She has been waging war in our home against dirt in any of its forms all of our married life. There is no way that she is going to let her quadriplegic husband look disheveled, dirty, unkempt, unshaved, or not dressed in the best and most appropriate outfit available. My wheelchair, which is such an extension of me, is dusted daily and cleaned. Even the wheels are checked to make sure they are spotless. Though not much to look at, I go out in public with great confidence, knowing that Jo Anne has made me as presentable as possible. Doctors and nurses are always amazed that I look and feel as good as I do. They stand in awe of the quality of care I have received at her hands for such a lengthy period of time. What I look like, and my attitude of faith and hope, really tell you much more about Jo Anne then they do of me.

I believe that cleanliness and orderliness and being in control of one's life are an important part of what life is all about. They communicate better than words what our true character really is. I know we can go overboard and be obsessed by appearance and style, but true cleanliness and orderliness are never out of style.

Dad / Grandpa / Jack

Life Is for
GIVING

ONE OF MY favorite musicals is *Les Misérables*. I have read Victor Hugo's book and seen several movie versions, as well as Andrew Lloyd Webber's musical production. In fact, Jo Anne and I went to see the play in Los Angeles as part of the celebration of our twenty-fifth wedding anniversary. Just a week after seeing the play, I had my accident at Laguna Beach. The music always tugs at my heart because of the tender memories it rekindles.

One of the scenes in the 1936 production has had a greater impact on me than any of the others I have seen. It was when Jean Valjean had stolen the priest's silver dishes and silverware, had been captured by the police, and was brought back to the priest's lodgings. Jean Valjean's life was changed forever when the priest assured the police that he had given the silver to him as a present. The police looked on in amazement as the priest walked over to two beautiful silver candlesticks above the mantle and told Jean Valjean that he must have forgotten them. He proceeded to place them in the bag along with the other silver items. The priest then said to Jean Valjean in a soft but penetrating voice as he intensely looked into his eyes, "Whenever you look at these candlesticks remember that *life is for giving and not taking!*" The confused but humbled Jean Valjean stumbled out into the night a changed man. The priest's words that "life is for giving and not taking" became the standard by which Jean Valjean governed his life from that moment on.

I have pondered that line for quite some time. During my lifetime, I have been the recipient of countless acts of kindness by many whose lives have been about giving and not taking. The addition to our home was built by men and women who only wanted to give and give. A good friend of ours, a professional wallpaper hanger, recently spent days in our home stripping old wallpaper and hanging some new. Years ago he volunteered to wallpaper our home and would not let us pay him. He is a master craftsman, and it is a joy to watch him magically transform a room, it seems to me, in just a matter of minutes. Jo Anne tried to pay him for his work this time, but he would not accept it. He did, however, agree to let us take him out to dinner—a small token for a job superbly done.

You know when somebody is doing something for you out of love and not just out of duty. Such an example is always humbling to me. It is but the tip of the iceberg of so many others who have given so selflessly over the years to bless our lives.

Visiting the Bob Freeman family.

I would be amiss not to mention another good friend who is Jo Anne's "SOS" man. He always seems to be on standby just in case Jo Anne calls, anytime, night or day. He has come to our rescue many times over the past twenty years. It does not seem to matter if the ramp on the van gets stuck or if my wheelchair breaks. He can usually fix it. Once when Jo Anne was out of town with her friend Kelli, I was left in the care of my youngest daughter, Jackie. One afternoon she had to take me with her to pick her daughter up from preschool. As we pulled in our driveway, the baby was crying and the toddler was complaining. It was very hectic as she tried to maneuver me out of the van—not an easy job for someone who doesn't do it all of the time. As she pulled me backward, my foot got caught and the leg rest on the wheelchair broke off, leaving my foot dangling. Amidst the crying children, Jackie immediately called her mother for help. Jo Anne, hundreds of miles away, said, "Call Ron Wilson. He will know what to do!" That he did. His neighbor was a welder, who just happened to be home as well (aren't we blessed?). Between the two of them, my leg rest was as good as new.

An unsettling thought constantly lurks in the back of my mind: *Am I more of a taker than a giver?* Whenever I see a doctor or a nurse, the first thing they do is take my vital signs. I always ask them if I am still alive. Once they realize I am not in imminent danger of passing on to the other side, they begin to address other issues.

It probably wouldn't be a bad idea to do a frequent checkup of our spiritual vital signs to see where we are on the "giving or taking" continuum. If the taking is alarmingly greater than the giving, we may be in imminent danger of spiritual death.

The parable of the good Samaritan has been expounded by many over the years. My take on it (but it's not my own original insight) is that it is a macro view of human nature with regard to giving and taking. The thieves that beat the poor man almost to death and took all his possessions had the attitude, "What is yours is mine if I am strong enough or smart enough to take it from you." The mind-set of the priest and Levite was, "What is mine is mine and I intend to keep it and not give it away." The attitude of the innkeeper was, "What is mine is yours if you have enough money to pay for it." And finally the good Samaritan felt that "What is mine is yours, and you are welcome to it and as much as you need for as long as you need."

I think we would all like to be like the good Samaritan, but because we are human, at times we are a composite of all these attitudes. Hopefully, by the end of the day we will be more like the good Samaritan than the other characters in the parable.

Of course, on the broad spectrum of giving and taking, Christ is on one end and Satan on the other. One is the great giver and the other the great taker. Satan wants to take everything from us as well as the glory from the Father. He is still trying to do that through evil people that follow his lead as takers. What did Christ give? He gave us our agency and the opportunity to inherit the greatest gift we can receive which is the gift of eternal life. In doing so he gave his life: "Greater love hath no man than this that a man lay down his life for his friends" (John 15:13).

I really do want to be more of a giver than a taker, but I'm not there yet. I hope that someday we will all fully realize and implement in our daily lives the truth communicated by the priest to Jean Valjean: "Life is for giving, not taking!"

Dad/Grandpa/Jack

The Invasion
OF THE ANTS

JO ANNE'S BIRTHDAY is on April Fools' Day. She is the fourth of ten children and is the oldest girl in her family. Being the first girl and born on April Fools' Day, she truly did fool her parents. There is no fooling, however, that Jo Anne has been a source of joy to all who have known her.

Of her many sterling qualities, two are very special and have impacted my life in a positive way over the years. She has been blessed with the ability to live life and serve others with unwearyingness. The word *unwearyingness* does not appear in my online dictionary, but I believe the meaning of the word is self-evident. It implies never giving up, being firm and steadfast, and enduring well to the end. I can think of no better word to describe Jo Anne.

Of the many examples I could give to support my claim, let me just share one. I sleep in a hospital bed downstairs, while Jo Anne occupies the master bedroom upstairs. We have a baby monitor in my room and a receiver in the dining room and the

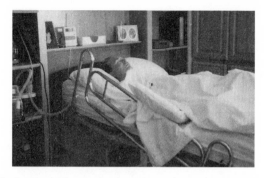

master bedroom. This system works well, and Jo Anne can hear any unusual sound emanating from my bedroom. Almost every night, usually after midnight when she is in a deep sleep, I need help. I speak in a normal voice into the baby monitor something like this: "Jo Anne, I hate to wake you up, but I really do need your help; it is not an emergency—don't panic—but if you could come down, it would be a great blessing because I'm not breathing really well." A minute or two will elapse, and then Jo Anne will almost magically appear at my bedside. At that time in the morning she looks a little scary, but she takes care of my need and then invariably asks if there is anything else she can do for me. She never makes me feel that I am imposing on her or that she is upset because I have awakened her out of a blissful and deep sleep. I believe one's true Christianity is severely tested in the early morning hours when required to leave a warm comfortable bed to see to the needs of another. Jo Anne has passed this test for many years with her unwearyingness.

Another trait that Jo Anne possesses in abundance is creativity. She is never content to simply maintain the status quo. She is constantly inventing new and better ways of caring for me. In fact, she has invented several different items that I think could be patented that have made her caring for me and the quality of my life so much better. Her creativity, however, reached its high point the morning of what I call the invasion of the ants.

It happened one summer morning a number of years ago. The day and night preceding the invasion were unusually hot. Ants seem to want to be as comfortable as we do, and so during the hot weather they will seek a cooler environment. When Jo Anne put me to bed that night, she left my windows partially open to let whatever cool breeze was available into my room. During the night the ant nation sent out some scouts to find food and a better environment for their friends and relatives. They somehow sensed that my bedroom window was open and, lucky for them, they found me. I'm sure the following conversation took place between the scouts: "Wow, look at the hunk of dead meat that we've found! If we can somehow get it home, it will feed everyone for years to come. It's going to take the entire nation, however, to accomplish this feat."

And so during the night, the entire ant nation invaded my bedroom and tried to carry me off. These ants were very smart and somehow sensed they shouldn't travel beyond my neck. Therefore, I slept blissfully through the night, unaware of the invasion.

In the morning, Jo Anne came in to turn me onto my back, and when she pulled the covers off, she saw that I was covered from my neck to my feet with ants. She screamed and then disappeared. A second later, she returned with a big can of Black Flag insect killer and proceeded to spray me and the ants with a generous amount of this poison. In a minute or two she had successfully annihilated the ant nation and had almost gotten rid of me as well. Again, she disappeared and quickly reappeared with her little vacuum cleaner (she is a vacuum junkie and always has a wide variety of vacuums on the premises). Using the hose attachment, she proceeded to vacuum up the dead ants from my body and the bed. Soon no evidence remained of the massacre of the ants, but the upside, as well as the downside, was that for the next week, no insect, pest, or human being would get very close to me. You just have to love a girl with that kind of creativity, don't you?

Thank you, Jo Anne, for your unwearyingness and creativity. And by the way, have a happy birthday—no fooling!

Dad / Grandpa / Jack

Blood for an
ENEMY

OUR SON JOHN is an ER doctor. The Air Force paid
for his education, and he agreed to serve in the Air Force
for three years, blessing wounded troops with the skills he
gained in medical school and his residency.

As mentioned earlier, John and his friend Matt, who were
sixteen at the time, were body surfing with me when I had my
accident. They were able to get me onto the beach and basically saved my life. As a teenager, John was very involved in
my care. He was the only kid in his high school that would say
to his friends most evenings, "I have to go home and put my
dad to bed."

Periodically, John would sleep in my bedroom with me,
which was downstairs, so Jo Anne could get a good night's
rest and not have to worry about my needs during the night.
I was always a little worried that John might not wake up
if I needed him, or that if he did, he wouldn't be coherent

enough to help me. One night I put him to the test. It was about 3:00 AM, and I was having problems breathing. The alarm sounded, and I waited for John to wake up and help me. I was sleeping on my side facing his bed across the room. I looked to him for help, but he didn't budge. I said to myself, "Here he is getting a good night's sleep, and I'm about to enter the spirit world!" In desperation I offered the following prayer: "Heavenly Father, please bless John to wake up and take care of this problem." I had no sooner offered the prayer than John leaped out of bed, ran across the room, picked up the phone, and said, "Hello."

John nearly lost his life once. When he was two years old, he swallowed a straight pin without us knowing it. He was very sick for several weeks and ran high fevers. The doctors could find no cause for his illness. They finally did X-rays and saw the pin in his abdomen. Further tests revealed a huge abscess that had formed on the liver, and immediate surgery followed. Apparently, after swallowing the pin, it penetrated the appendix and lodged there. After a period of time, the trapped pin began to rust, and the appendix became infected and sent the poison to the liver. After the abscess was drained and the appendix removed, John lay in a hospital crib with IVs and other tubes hooked to him for nearly a month. During all that time, he lay at death's door until a last resort medication was administered that had severe side effects. It did the trick, left no aftermath, and we were finally able to take him home. I always found it ironic

Jack and Jo Anne with their son John, an ER doctor.

that John, who nearly lost his life, saved my life on the beach that day. And now as an ER doctor, he is prepared to save other people's lives as well.

When John was in the Air Force, each year he was deployed to a different part of the world. His first deployment was a big army base outside of Kabul, Afghanistan. He and two other ER doctors managed the ER unit twenty-four hours a day, seven days a week. Part of their duty was to take turns going out in helicopters to pick up the wounded.

After his first helicopter experience, he wrote the following email:

Hey Dad and family,

So things are going well here. I went on my first helicopter mission a few days ago. It was pretty exciting. We had to go pick up an enemy combatant who was shot while trying to set up an IED (improvised explosive device). We flew about an hour to where the patient was being held. He was shot in the bottom while bent over setting up a bomb, but the bullet went into his stomach and hurt his intestines and nicked a big artery in his pelvis. By the time I saw him he had already gone through 11 units of blood, which was the entire supply of blood at that base. Throughout the chopper ride back, I had to monitor his vitals and had to keep giving him drugs to keep him sedated.

We flew really close to the ground, about 200 feet. The surrounding area is really pretty and you would never know there was a war going on. There are a lot of rivers and farms, kids playing soccer, etc. In the helicopter were myself, 2 pilots, and 2 soldiers looking out both sides of the helicopter for possible enemies on the ground. Behind us we had a big black hawk helicopter loaded with guns that was covering us in case we came under fire. I was a little nervous on the flight to get the patient, but on the way back I was so busy keeping him stabilized that I didn't have time to think about the dangers.

It's pretty amazing the effort we make to take care of the enemy. I don't think they would do the same for us. I mean the guy got all the blood at that one base. If one of our soldiers had gotten hurt, there would not have been any blood for them. Also just think of the risk involved in just going to pick the wounded enemy up. When we arrived with the patient, we discovered we were also out of B- blood and we actually had to get volunteers to give their blood to this guy who was essentially trying to kill us. I think it says something really special about this country that we would put so much effort into saving people like this.

Reading John's email made me feel proud to be an American. Imagine risking your life and giving your blood to an enemy seeking to take your life. Anyone who says we don't value human life and freedom in this country is wrong!

Many of the pundits in Washington D.C. could benefit from reading John's email. Even though many are opposed to our involvement in Iraq and Afghanistan and believe President Bush got into the war on terrorism prematurely, it's refreshing to know that we are actively striving to do something good in the world and that we place such a high value on human life, dignity, freedom, and liberty.

Our land is filled with a spirit of pessimism and negativity. Since 9/11, we feel we have been put upon as a nation. Can you even imagine what it would have been like to live in England at the beginning of World War II when Nazi Germany had overrun most of Europe and was threatening to invade England as well? Thankfully for Western civilization, there was a Winston Churchill who was the essence of optimism and courage. He rallied the people as no one else could in that dark and desperate time. In speaking at Harrow School, which he had attended as a boy, he said: "Do not let us speak of darker days; let us speak rather of sterner days. These are not dark days: these are great days—the greatest days our country has ever lived; and we must all thank God that we have been allowed, each of us according to our stations, to play a part in making these days memorable in the history of our race."[1]

Following the disaster at Dunkirk when the prophets of doom were foretelling disaster and the imminent demise of the British Empire, Churchill provided these stirring words for his countrymen: "We shall not flag or fail. . . . We shall fight in France, we shall fight on the seas and oceans, we shall fight with growing confidence and growing strength in the air, we shall defend our island, whatever the cost may be, we shall fight on the beaches, we shall fight on the landing grounds, we shall fight in the fields and in the streets, we shall fight in the hills; we shall never surrender."

We need the spirit of Winston Churchill today in this country. Our way of life—the way of life that inspires us to give our blood to the enemy to save his life—must be preserved at any cost. You may not agree with the war on terrorism or our current president's decisions, but it's hard to deny that we have entered a battle with an evil ideology that will rob us of everything we hold dear.

Thank you, John, for reminding us that we belong to a pretty special country!

Dad/Grandpa/Jack

Notes
1. Address at Harrow School, Oct. 29, 1941.
2. Speech on Dunkirk, House of Commons, June 4, 1940.

Eating—Blessing or
CURSE?

I HATE TO admit it, but eating has become my favorite indoor and outdoor sport. Since I can't do much of anything else physically, I love to eat! Jo Anne and I were at a wedding reception one evening and were sitting at a table with some friends we hadn't seen for many years. Jo Anne was shoveling pasta, Caesar salad, and rolls into my mouth as my friend watched in amazement. "Don't you have any restrictions to your diet in your condition?" Between bites of pasta and salad, I managed to choke out the words, "Only what Jo Anne places on me." My statement to my friend, I'm sorry to report, had grave implications.

After my accident, I had a feeding tube inserted in my stomach and was on a ventilator system that did not allow me to speak, eat, or drink. I was so traumatized by what was happening that I can't say I missed eating regular food. The nutrients that came to me through the feeding tube seemed to satisfy my need for nourishment, and I wasn't suffering from hunger pangs.

About a month and a half after the feeding tube had been

inserted, the doctor felt it was time for me to eat normally again. It's hard to believe now that I had no desire to eat once the feeding tube was removed. Nothing tasted good to me, and eating was simply a bother. I believe I was also in a deep depression and simply could not eat. Every mealtime became a confrontation between Jo Anne and me—she pushing food on me I didn't want and me resisting vigorously. Finally, the doctor threatened to put the feeding tube back in, which would have caused me to take a big step backward in my recovery.

The Vita Mix machine came to the rescue. I could easily suck through a straw, whereas chewing required more energy and power than I could muster at the time. Jo Anne and her dad began concocting wonderful Vita Mix drinks with every conceivable nutritious food in them, including protein supplements. I would manage to get down a couple of those each day.

I still remember the day Jo Anne and I were going down one of the corridors at Rancho Los Amigos Hospital and I felt hunger pangs for the first time in months. There was a food cart in that part of the hospital, and if I remember correctly, Jo Anne bought me a burrito that tasted better than good.

Once I started eating again, I grew accustomed to it rather quickly. Everything became delicious to me. When Jo Anne and I ran errands, we would invariably stop at Carl's Jr. to pick me up a Western Bacon Cheeseburger with fries. Jo Anne felt sorry for me at the time and didn't know how long I would live, so she was willing to meet all of my requests for greasy hamburgers and fries.

One day my son John looked at me closely and said,

"Mom, don't you think Dad is getting really fat?" I never did like that kid! Jo Anne took a critical look at me and instantaneously escorted me out of hamburger heaven. She put me on a diet, and when I'm on a diet, I can't cheat. Think  about it. For many years now, every item of food that has entered my mouth has come by way of Jo Anne, or under her direction. In the midst of one of my first "Jo Anne diets," Dick Fox, a good friend, saved my life. Jo Anne left me in his care one afternoon, and Dick cunningly smuggled into our house a brown paper bag filled with bite-size Snickers, a can of sour cream Pringles, and a large can of cashews. I thought I had died and gone to heaven.

I have learned to eat in a variety of positions. For example, I eat really well flat on my back. A couple years ago when I was in intensive care, I ordered bacon and eggs, hash browns, and pancakes for breakfast. I was lying flat on my back, and an elderly RN refused to feed me until she could prop me up. I finally convinced her that I could handle breakfast efficiently in my current position. She was astonished as I inhaled that big breakfast. However, I don't do so well on my left or right side. Soup is a particular problem when lying on my side. Jo Anne is not extremely good with her left hand, and as she spoons clam chowder into my mouth with an awkward backhand motion, I get about a third of the spoonful in my mouth, and the rest runs down my chin. Have you ever had a clam chowder bath?

I do my best eating when I'm sitting in my wheelchair. It has been very interesting not being able to feed myself how and when I would like to. Eating lunch with Jo Anne at home, for example, can take an inordinate amount of time. She will give me a bite of sandwich and then check the mail. If there's mail, she will take it into her office and go through it. Then she'll whiz through the kitchen and give me another bite on her way to put in a load of wash. And so it goes. If I have soup, halfway through lunch she has to reheat it. I don't want to put Jo Anne in a bad light, however. She has been blessed with a great talent for multitasking. She can feed me, herself, and a granddaughter seated on her lap all at the same time without missing a beat.

You can tell a lot about a person by the way they feed you. If we to go to a restaurant or have a special meal at home, Jo Anne invariably gives me the first bite. I often wonder if I would do the same.

In all honesty, Jo Anne has helped preserve the quality of my life through her wise choices and the food she allows me to eat. I consider her my personal fitness trainer and submit my will to hers regarding my diet. With my weight under control and with Jo Anne getting a bit softer, you might see us at In-N-Out Burger more frequently than you would imagine.

Dad/Grandpa/Jack

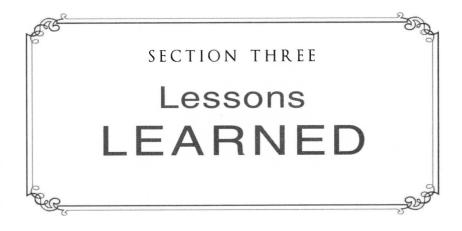

SECTION THREE

Lessons
LEARNED

We Was
ROBBED!

I THINK I first heard the phrase "We was robbed!" as a young boy when I became a dyed in the wool, true blue through and through, Dodgers fan. They were then the Brooklyn Dodgers and had the uncanny habit of snatching defeat from the jaws of victory on a regular basis. However, they never owned up to the fact that it was their own fault and ineptitude that the Yankees always beat them in the World Series, or that the Giants came from thirteen games behind to snatch the pennant from them on a sad September afternoon many years ago. Why couldn't I have been a Yankee fan? Life would have been so much more pleasant over the years, but I got stuck with the Dodgers.

After blowing yet another game, the Dodgers inevitably would excuse themselves by saying, "We was robbed!" In other words, the umpires were against them, there were too many bad hops, the baseballs were doctored up, the

Yankees had all the money, the pitcher was throwing up spitballs, and so on.

The "we was robbed" mentality weakens us and keeps us from achieving our true potential. Without realizing it, sometimes parents promote this kind of thinking in their children. Parents mistakenly think it is the coach's fault that their athletically gifted child is not starting and sits on the bench. It is the teacher's fault that their intelligent child is not getting straight A's. It is the piano teacher's fault that their child prodigy is having difficulty playing "Twinkle, Twinkle, Little Star."

My son Rich is an avid Dodgers, Lakers, and UCLA basketball fan. I couldn't have had any influence on him in that regard when he was just a little kid, could I? John R. Wooden, the former great UCLA basketball coach, and arguably the greatest basketball coach of all time, is one of our all-time favorite heroes. Rich sent me an email with a quote from Coach Wooden's book, *Wooden: A Lifetime of Observations and Reflections On and Off the Court.*

In the book, Wooden shared some advice his father gave to him as a young boy that influenced his life forever, both as a basketball coach and as a human being. It was simply this: "Don't whine, don't complain, and don't make excuses."

Of course, this philosophy is the antithesis of "we was robbed!" I can't help but think Coach Wooden's philosophy of not complaining, whining, or making excuses will take us a lot further in life than thinking "we was robbed."

In the late sixties, I taught religious education at the Utah

State Industrial School in Ogden, Utah, for three years. This school was actually a coed prison/reform school for juvenile delinquents. Those students were some of the most depressed young people I had ever encountered. They had totally bought into the "we was robbed" mentality. It is true that for the most part they had less than wonderful parents and came from dysfunctional homes. Using this and many other negative things in their lives as excuses for their lawless and dangerous behavior, and the inevitable misery that followed, very few of them would ever take ownership for their unhappy lives. They all had the same goal, which was to get out of the Utah State Industrial School so they could be free and happy.

The facility did not have a high-security system, and these kids were extremely creative in escaping and running to "freedom and joy." Within a week, or at most a month, they would return to the school, worse off and more miserable than when they ran. They constantly whined, complained, and made excuses for their bad behavior and resulting misery because they felt "they was robbed."

We tried desperately to teach them the following significant truth about life: the way out is the way through. They wanted out of misery and out of the reform school so they could have freedom and joy. Few of them ever got the message that they couldn't run from their problems and that the only way to freedom was to deal with them.

It is much easier to teach a great truth than to live it. After my accident, I found myself slipping into the "we was robbed" mentality. I felt I had been robbed of my body, my vocation as a teacher, my church service, and my ability to be an effective husband, father, and grandfather.

Eventually, the principle I had taught my juvenile delinquents so many years before came into my mind and heart: "Jack, the only way out is the way through!"

Immediately after the accident, the neurosurgeons told me I had suffered a complete injury to my spinal cord. It had been severed and there was absolutely no possibility that I would ever get mobility or feeling back. It took months and even years to accept this truth. I tried to run and escape from the prison that had become my body, even as my reform school kids had done from their prison. Eventually I was able to empathize more fully with their challenge.

Finally, the day came that I could say to myself, "Jack, you are paralyzed from the neck down and are on life support. That is the way you will be the rest of today, tomorrow, next week, next month, and for as long as you live." When I was able to admit that, I began to work my way out of misery and find the freedom and joy I longed to have.

The "we was robbed" mentality, coupled with whining, complaining, and finding excuses for our unhappiness is a one-way street to nowhere. This thought reminds me of a scripture from the book of Proverbs: "A merry heart doeth good like a medicine: but a broken spirit drieth the bones" (Proverbs 17:22).

The other day, Jo Anne and I spoke to a woman from our church who has cancer and is undergoing chemotherapy.

Jo Anne commented that she sounded like the healthiest and happiest person in town. This woman's affliction is serious and painful, but she has chosen to have an attitude of faith and hope. It was always a delight to visit with her before her struggle with cancer, and it is even more a delight now because of her merry heart.

Jenkin Lloyd Jones once wrote:

> Anyone who imagines that bliss is normal, is going to waste a lot of time running around shouting that he's been robbed. Most putts don't drop. Most beef is tough. Most children grow up to be just people. Most successful marriages require a high degree of mutual toleration. Most jobs are more often dull than otherwise. Life is like an old-time rail journey—delays, sidetracks, smoke, dust, cinders, and jolts, interspersed only occasionally by beautiful vistas and thrilling bursts of speed. The trick is to thank the Lord for letting you have the ride.[1]

I, for one, believe life has been a wonderful ride, in spite of some "delays, sidetracks, smoke, dust, cinders, and jolts." No matter our circumstances, we really should just thank the Lord for letting us have the ride.

Dad / Grandpa / Jack

Note
1. Jenkin Lloyd Jones, *Deseret News*, June 12, 1973.

Wisdom
TEETH

SOME TIME AGO, Jo Anne had our dermatologist look at a sore on my arm that would not heal. I was happy to go, knowing that I couldn't feel whatever he did to me from the neck on down. When the problem is from the neck up— something that occurs far too often—I get nervous because I know that it will hurt. The dermatologist looked at my hand and had the nurse prepare a surgical tray to biopsy the affected area. On the tray was a hypodermic needle with some kind of medication to numb the sore that he was about to cut. Before he began, I assured him I didn't need to have my hand numbed because I couldn't feel anything. He asked me if I was sure, and I told him I definitely was, so he hesitantly did not give me the shot. Never having been paralyzed, he could not conceive not being able to experience pain.

While I watched, he took such a large hunk out of my arm that he had to give me quite a few stitches. The nurse bandaged me all up, and for being a good boy, Jo Anne took me to In-N-Out Burger. The nurse called a few days later and said the lab had confirmed that it was skin cancer but that the doctor had removed all the dangerous tissue. I guess I will have to find some other way to exit mortality.

Not being able to feel pain is both a blessing and a liability. On the one hand, having no feeling is really quite convenient when I have kidney stones, ingrown toe nails, and minor surgeries performed on my lower anatomy. Not needing any pain-numbing medication, I have chatted with doctors as they have cut away on me, which was always a bit distracting and uncomfortable for them. I think they would have rather operated on someone who was comatose.

As the years have gone by however, I have felt it has been more of a liability. Not being able to feel pain, I don't know when I am being hurt and can't take the steps to protect myself from further harm. Several years ago, my daughter's young friend, Doug Barbour, was showing off a little as he was helping me get into our modified van. As he pushed me rapidly into place, the ring finger on my left hand was caught on the back of the driver's seat. As I watched it bend all the way back to my wrist, I said to myself, "Boy, I'll bet that hurts!" Sure enough, the finger turned black and blue and swelled up, so Jo Anne hauled me off to the doctor to have it X-rayed. The doctor came in with the X-ray and said, "Well, Mr. Rushton, your finger is fractured, and we are going to have to immobilize it." "Immobilize it?" I thought to myself. I wondered where this guy had gone to medical school.

Speaking of feeling pain, I hate to admit it, but I am not nearly as wise today as I was a couple of days ago. I had to go to an oral surgeon to have two wisdom teeth extracted.

When I was a young married man, I let a dentist in Ogden, Utah, talk me into pulling all my wisdom teeth. As it turned out, it was not a very wise decision on my part. He started in the afternoon, and by 8:00 PM I was still in the chair and only the two wisdom teeth on the right side of my mouth had been pulled. As he was working on me, he would say things like, "Oops, I think maybe I shouldn't have done it that way." He wanted to make an appointment to pull out the wisdom teeth on the left side, but for some reason I did not feel inclined to take him up on his offer. He said that at some point in time, those remaining wisdom teeth would become a problem. I never wanted to see the fulfillment of his prophecy, and since then, one of my life's goals was to die before the wisdom teeth went bad on me. No such luck!

In all honesty, it was a brutal experience. Several times during the procedure I wanted to cry, but old men are supposed to be tough. So I stifled the desire to scream, moan, and groan, and suffered in silence. The longer the tooth extraction took, the more the oral surgeon began to look like a hairy, muscle bound, eight-hundred-pound gorilla who was trying to pull my head off.

I hate to admit it, but during this seemingly never-ending procedure, I was only thinking about myself and my pain and misery. With the oral surgeon's hands in my mouth, along with his various instruments of torture, I was not very concerned about those troops who had been recently killed at Fort Hood, Texas, and their surviving families and loved ones, or the thousands that have been killed in recent earthquakes and tsunamis, or the poor starving children in Africa, or even some dear friends who are suffering from severe health problems much worse than mine. I was only thinking about one thing—me!

I felt the same way when I suffered my injury many years ago. I was consumed with "me." I was totally self-absorbed in my pain, and in that condition I could not reach out to help others or even be concerned with their unique challenges.

I take comfort in the fact that I think all of us, because of our humanness, are much the same way. Victor Frankl, the author of *Man's Search for Meaning*, drew the following parallel regarding the relativity of human suffering: "A man's suffering is similar to the behavior of gas. If a certain quantity of gas is pumped into an empty chamber, it will fill the chamber completely and evenly, no matter how big the chamber. Thus suffering completely fills the human soul and conscious mind, no matter whether the suffering is great or little. Therefore the 'size' of human suffering is absolutely relative."

Frankl is saying that if I am having wisdom teeth pulled out in California while people in Fort Hood, Texas, are being slaughtered by a maniacal killer, or the good folks in Samoa or Peru are losing their lives because of earthquakes and tsunamis, I am going to be much more concerned with my pain than theirs. Like Victor Frankl, I believe that each individual's suffering—regardless of the kind or "size"—can completely fill his soul and conscious mind, leaving little room to be concerned about the miseries of others. Because of this, I also believe one of the challenges we all face is to rise above our own self-abosrbing pain and misery and reach out emotionally and spiritually to help others in need.

The English writer John Donne (1572–1631), in one of his most famous essays, "Meditation 17," from "Devotions Upon Emergent Occasions," wrote, "No man is an island, entire of itself; every man is a piece of the continent, a part of the main. If a clod be washed away by the sea, Europe is the less. . . . Any man's death diminishes me because I am involved in mankind; and therefore never send to know for whom the bell tolls; it tolls for thee."

As I think about Donne's words, I cannot help but think of the suffering all of God's children experience while on this earth. As we struggle with our own pain and observe the pain and suffering of others, we have several options available to us. We could pretend that we don't see the suffering of others. At our worst, we could take advantage of the sick and weak and take from them what little resources they may have. On the other hand, we could give of our means and time to bless the unfortunate around us.

One thing I know for sure, based on my own personal experience, is that none of us will ever successfully make it alone without the love and support of others. We need one another! Truly, "no man is an island." Without my family and friends, and their love and support that has been constant since the day of my injury, I would certainly have perished long ago.

When the hairy, eight-hundred-pound gorilla comes into your life and tries to pull your head off, I hope you can see beyond your own pain and misery and reach out to bless others. If you do, you'll find that you're blessing yourself as well.

Dad/Grandpa/Jack

Illusion vs.
REALITY

SEVERAL YEARS AGO, Jo Anne and I went to a movie entitled *The Illusionist*. The main character was a master magician who was able to create illusions that seemed very real to his audiences. He was so skillful that those who attended his performance could not distinguish reality from the fiction he created. It was quite an entertaining movie and started me thinking about the concept of illusions. The world we live in is full of illusions and the illusionists that create them.

I believe the first and possibly most blatant illusionist I have ever encountered was a fellow I worked with the summer I drove truck for Kennecott Copper Corporation at the Liberty Pit in Ruth, Nevada, where I grew up. I worked the graveyard shift—11:30 PM to 7:30 AM. Every night just before we began our shift a man would drive into the parking lot in a beautiful Cadillac. He was always dressed in an immaculate blue suit, a sparkling white shirt, a gorgeous tie, and the shiniest shoes imaginable. To top it off, he also wore a very expensive gray hat and had a large cigar clamped between his teeth.

Being an innocent youth, I asked one of my fellow truck drivers if this man was the president of Kennecott Copper Corporation. My friend laughed and said, "Keep an eye on him and see what happens."

The man in the blue suit disappeared into the locker room, and in a moment or two, he emerged looking like the rest of us, wearing coveralls and old beat-up shoes. I was astonished when instead of mounting one of the huge earth-movers we were all driving, he climbed into the water truck. His job, the easiest and most mundane at Liberty Pit, was to drive around and sprinkle the dirt roads to keep the dust in check. At the end of the shift, he again disappeared into the locker room and emerged as he had entered eight hours earlier. I am sure his neighbors and other acquaintances believed he was at the very least the vice-president of the Ely, Nevada, Last National Bank.

His illusion was harmless, but as I have thought about this experience over the years, it has occurred to me that many of us wear a "blue suit." We are tempted to appear to be what we are not—deceiving others and oftentimes even ourselves. Sad to say, during every election year, a number of illusionists run for public office, many of whom strive to intellectually deceive or mislead us. We must work hard at discerning the truth from the illusion. How wonderful it is to know people who are not illusionists, but who are exactly what they appear to be.

While in high school, my oldest son, Mike, was the starting running back for the football team. He was in great shape and was working hard lifting weights and running. One morning as I was leaving for work, I saw Mike standing in front of the big mirror in the bathroom downstairs by the front door. He was flexing his muscles, posing, and obviously admiring what he saw. He had six pack abs and looked great. As I walked out the front door, I felt prompted to say, "Mike, if the day ever comes that you spend as much time developing your mind and spirit as you are now spending on developing your body,

Mike and his family at his enrobement ceremony.

you will be awesome." Mike is now a judge on the Riverside County, California Superior Court and, in my mind, he is truly awesome. His life is evidence to me of the law of the harvest. He reaped what he sowed and is definitely no illusionist.

What about teachers? I am quite sensitive about this, having been a teacher for most of my life. For twenty-five years I was able to rub shoulders with many great educators who influenced me greatly by their examples of integrity and fine teaching. Thankfully, even now in my wheelchair, I have opportunities to teach. In fact, I always tell my students that I am the most laid back teacher they will ever have. I don't write on the chalkboard and never use visual aids. Not wanting to be guilty of being an illusionist, I try to do in-depth preparations and ponder deeply the things I want to teach. In doing so I am just following in the footsteps of my two older brothers, who were both master teachers. I was thrilled when my daughter, Jo Lene, became a teacher. She is now teaching English as a second language (ESL) to adults from other countries and backgrounds trying to make their way in America. Jo Lene, like my brothers, has dedicated her life to helping others learn and to make the world a better place.

When my son, Richard, was fourteen years old, I had the opportunity (I use that word loosely) of going with him and eleven other Boy Scouts on a survival hike. A young man by the name of Bob Hoskisson, who had been a survival instructor at a university, was to take us out by Escalante, Utah, near Lake Powell. He was very familiar with the terrain as he had taken many groups of students there to live off the land for a month. As the day of departure grew near, various scout leaders began finding excuses for not going. It reminded me a great deal of rats abandoning ship. We only ended up with four adult leaders—me, Bob Hoskisson, another father, and a faithful friend of mine.

We each got to take a wool blanket, a few clothes, and a sandwich bag each of flour, raisins, powdered milk, and rice. To that we added several pieces of cheese, two bouillon

cubes, a carrot, a potato, and a canteen. Once we arrived, Bob started down the canyon without looking back at us. The hike turned out to be pure survival. During the days of this experience, Bob demonstrated that he

was a cross between Superman and Daniel Boone. He was no illusionist, and we knew it. Our very lives were in his hands, and he was more than capable of leading us to safety.

In my own life, I have always tried to discern the difference between an illusionist and the real thing. Like our survival hike, it can be a matter of life or death. One hot summer day a vein in my stomach hemorrhaged, and I literally lay bleeding to death. As I was surrounded by my loved ones, Dr. Nakano, a female doctor I had never met before, whispered in my ear, "Jack, if I don't operate now you will die!" As I lay there, nearly unconscious, I thought, "She looked like a doctor and talked like a doctor." I could sense she was not wearing a "blue suit" and I simply said, "Do it!" She knew what she was doing because of years of arduous study and work and proved to be a blessing in saving my life.

As a young fourteen-year-old, I was on the state of Nevada's championship American Legion baseball team. Before playing in the western regional tournament, our coaches scheduled a doubleheader with a team from Utah to keep us in practice. Because we were already the champions, we didn't take the game too seriously and the team from Utah beat us twice. We just laughed it off and still thought we were pretty good even after being beat by a no-name team. That night when I got home, my dad was waiting for me at the back gate. He put his arm around my shoulders and said, "When you put on that uniform, you are supposed to be a baseball player. If you are not going to play as hard as you can and play to win, then don't put on the uniform."

Since that time I have had to wear many uniforms—that of a student, a missionary, a soldier in the National Guard, a teacher, a husband and father, and a church leader. Then twenty years ago I put on a uniform I couldn't have imagined ever wearing—that of a quadriplegic on life support. I hope if I am ever tempted to quit or not play hard, I will remember my dad's words and wear my uniform with dignity.

Perhaps one of the great challenges of life is not to create illusions in our own minds, somehow convincing ourselves we are something we really are not and have not paid the price to be. Appearance seems to have replaced substance in so many aspects of our society and lives. We spend so much time, money, and effort decorating ourselves and our homes that at times we forget to appropriately decorate our minds and souls.

Of course the master illusionist is Satan—the great deceiver. He would have us believe, for example, that wickedness can bring us happiness. This is in complete opposition to the eternal truth that wickedness never was happiness because it is contrary to the nature of the righteousness which is in God. And yet, through the ages, how many sorry people have bought into this illusion?

I believe the daily challenge we all face is to separate truth from illusion, especially to not deceive ourselves regarding ourselves.

Dad/Grandpa/Jack

Live Today, Learn
FOREVER

SEVERAL YEARS AGO at my oldest grandson's high school graduation, I was deeply impressed by a quote one of the student speakers shared. Quoting Gandhi, she said, "Live as though you are going to die tomorrow; learn as though you are going to live forever!" I thought that important truth was applicable to the graduates as they embarked on life's adventure. Of course, such a principle should govern each of our lives, regardless of our age or station in life.

Gandhi's statement attracted my attention because of my own experiences. Since living on life support for many years, and having had a number of near-death experiences because of it, I am very aware of how fragile my own life is. Because of this I describe my lifestyle as "living on the edge." However, as I have thought about it over the years, I truly do believe that all of us are living on the edge and have no guarantee of what tomorrow will bring. I know how true James's statement is: "Whereas ye know not what shall be on the morrow. For

With oldest grandson,
Michael Rushton, at his
high school graduation.

what is your life? *It is even a vapor, that appeareth for a little time, and then vanisheth away"* (James 4:14; emphasis added).

If what James says is true, then we should take Gandhi's advice seriously. It could have a profound impact on the way we live each day. Does living our lives "as though we are going to die tomorrow" mean that we should strive to pack every waking hour with more fun, golf, exciting experiences, travel, cruises, and so on? I don't think so. Don't get me wrong. I certainly do believe there is a place for all of the things that can bring us pleasure, but I have learned that at the end of the day the only thing that really matters is the quality of our relationships with our family, friends, and especially God.

I learned this important truth as I was stretched out on a hospital bed in a trauma unit and was told I would never move my body again, breathe on my own again, speak again, eat regular food again, or live outside a care facility. Having lost the use of my physical body, in that moment I realized that nothing I had done in my life really mattered much, except the relationships I had forged with my loved ones over the years.

With life as fragile as it is, I would think that every day we would want to strive to be kinder, less judgmental, more loving to all we know, and strive to follow the Lord's admonition, "As I have loved you, love one another" (John 15:12).

I also have strong feelings about the second part of the Gandhi statement: "Learn as though you are going to live forever!" I can somewhat understand what it might be like to enter a world where we no longer have a physical body. For many years now my life has basically been a life of the mind and spirit. I cannot adequately express how important knowledge is, especially gospel knowledge and a love for the scriptures and other good books that I had stored up in my mind and heart before my accident. Because of my immobile situation, I am now privileged to spend hours each day learning and discovering new truths. I suspect I have read more great books and learned more in the last twenty years, than in any other twenty-year period of my life.

I am thankful for a multitude of things, but very high on the list is my ability to read. Through reading I have become acquainted with some of the greatest people and the best minds that have ever lived, and have vicariously experienced many of the world's most important events in history. Isn't it incredible what twenty-six little letters can do?

Dr. Lowell L. Bennion wrote:

Jack with his sip 'n' puff reading machine.

A medical doctor once told me that the saddest patients he has are not the physically disabled, but those who didn't use their minds when they were young. He explained that the body breaks down, but the mind just gets richer as we go through life as we keep it alive, like a muscle. He encouraged people to get excited about some intellectual dimension of life. He then admonished for everyone to "Read, read, read, and think, think, think," promising if they did so that life would still be good even when the body breaks down.

Samuel Clemens (Mark Twain) once observed: "The man who can read and doesn't, is no better off than the man who can't read." I wholeheartedly agree with Mark Twain. In my own mind, to quit learning is to quit living!

Dad/Grandpa/Jack

Note

1. Lowell L. Bennion, *The Best of Lowell L. Bennion: Selected Writings, 1928–1988.* Edited by Eugene England. (Salt Lake City: Deseret Bock, 1988), 35.

If Rushton Can Do It,
ANYONE CAN DO IT!

I RECENTLY LISTENED to *Masters of the Sky*, by Donald L. Miller. It is a wonderful history of the Eighth United States Air Force stationed in England and flying bombing missions over Germany during World War II. I think I enjoyed the book so much because of my good friend Allen Rozsa. As a twenty-year-old, he was a pilot of one of the flying fortresses making bombing runs over Germany. Allen went on to make the Air Force his career and was a lieutenant colonel, in line to become a general when he took an early retirement. When I was in the rehabilitation hospital for six months following my injury, Allen was a frequent visitor and spent many hours at my bedside encouraging me. My son John, who was instrumental in saving my life at the ocean, would spend most Sundays with me so his mom could stay home with his young sisters. Our favorite thing to do was to get Allen to tell us war stories about his experiences

Jack in Guatemala.

of flying over Germany as a young man. Believe me, it was exciting, and John and I loved it.

As I have contemplated what Allen has been through, I have thought of my own puny contribution to the defense of our nation many years ago. I was sent to do my basic training at Fort Ord, California, in January of 1962. When I went to Fort Ord, I was a physical wreck. I had recently recovered from infectious hepatitis, which I had contracted while working with the Mayan Indian people in the highlands of Guatemala. I had spent forty-three days in a hospital in Guatemala City, and when I was released, I was so weak I could barely walk. I arrived home barely weighing 150 pounds, if that. I was pale and unable to do more than two or three push-ups at a time. I don't think I could do a sit-up, and pull-ups were impossible. In that kind of shape, I flew to San Francisco and was bused to Fort Ord to begin my basic training.

It was just my luck to be assigned to Company B 2-1. The company commander was a young man by the name of Lieutenant Squatriglia, who was an expert in jungle warfare and hand-to-hand combat. The army was his life. As my son Mike would say, he was an army Nazi. He was in great shape and even had muscles on his head. His uniform was spotless and so starched that you could have cut your hand by rubbing the creases on his pants. Even his underwear was khaki colored.

The first day he met me, we were all standing in line waiting to go into the mess hall to eat lunch. He was standing at the door, and as we approached him one by one, he would have us do as many push-ups as we could before entering and eating. I assumed the correct position and cranked out three great push-ups. To say the least, Lieutenant Squatriglia was less than impressed. He just knew that I could do more than I was doing and couldn't believe there could be anybody as weak as I appeared to be. From that day until the end of basic training, he made sure that I was the last person to enter the mess hall to eat. He didn't like anything about me. I wasn't "regular army" and he knew it. I was what they called a "six-month wonder." He took it upon himself to make my life as miserable as he could.

In turn, I did everything I could to upset him. I don't know why, but I secretly enjoyed infuriating Lieutenant Squatriglia. When we marched, I purposely marched a half step slower than everybody else with Lieutenant Squatriglia right at my side, counting the cadence loudly into my ear.

When we had bayonet training, he would stand in front of us and holler, "What is the spirit of the bayonet?" We were supposed to holler back enthusiastically, "To kill, to kill!" Then he would scream at us, "What two kinds of bayonet fighters are there?" We were supposed to scream back, "The quick and the dead!" He would then scream,

"What kind are you?" We were to holler back, "The quick!" And then he would shout at us, "What kind are they?" We were to shout back, "The dead!" Then we were supposed to growl like tigers. I just couldn't get into the spirit of the bayonet and always remained at the back of the group, not really shouting or growling. Lieutenant Squatriglia was well aware of this. It just killed him.

Lieutenant Squatriglia's greatest desire was for his company to do better than any other company at Fort Ord in the graded test that culminated our basic training. It was a series of ten events with a possible ten points on each event. I determined in my heart that I would get 100 percent on the graded test. Without Lieutenant Squatriglia realizing it, I was beginning to put on weight and was getting stronger through all the physical exertion and good food. I maintained a low profile, however, and tried to stay out of his way as best I could.

The day of the graded test came. My group's first event was at the rifle range. We had practiced shooting on a number of different occasions, but now we were shooting to qualify in different categories, the highest being "expert." You had to shoot expert to receive the maximum ten points in that particular event. The old M1 rifles we were using had a peep sight on them similar to the one on the rifle in *Quigley Down Under*. It seemed to be made just for me.

We were standing in foxholes with our rifles resting on a sandbag. Silhouette targets of men would pop up at different distances. I would squeeze the trigger, and they would fall down almost every time. It was incredible. It was one of the most enjoyable activities in which I had ever participated. When the results came in, I was one of the few men in the company who had qualified as expert on the rifle range.

I went from event to event, getting the maximum number of points each time. One of the events, for example, was throwing a dummy hand grenade through a swinging tire ten times. I put it through every single time. Another was crawling on your belly while cradling your rifle in your arms under a barbwire obstacle course in a specified amount of time.

By the end of the day, I knew that I had received 100 percent on every event. It took until evening for all of the results to be tabulated. When Lieutenant Squatriglia saw what I had done, he thought that I had somehow cheated and had the scorekeepers double check all of my scores. When he finally realized that everything was in proper order, he called the entire company of more than two hundred men onto the parade ground in front of our barracks. In all of Fort Ord in that particular cycle of basic training, only two men out of several thousand had earned 100 percent on the graded test. Lieutenant Squatriglia called out my name and had me stand in front of the entire company. He told them that I had received 100 percent on the graded test and then said, "This just goes to show, men, that if Rushton can do it, anybody can do it!"

Jack and his family after his release from
the military.

I have shared these experiences with you for a couple
of reasons. I believe the Lord knew I wouldn't do well in
Korea, Vietnam, or the Middle East. He let me do my duty
to my country at Fort Ord and then at the Presidio of San
Francisco. Based on my experience at Fort Ord, I learned to
be careful in judging others by their outward appearance.
You can never be sure what an individual is capable of or
what is in his heart.

Truer words were never spoken than, "If Rushton can
do it, anybody can do it!" A number of people have told me
that they could never endure what I have. That is not true!
We never know what we are capable of doing until we are
put to the test. And believe me, "If Rushton can do it, anybody can do it!"

Dad / Grandpa / Jack

Are You
LISTENING?

JO ANNE TOOK me to Costco awhile back to see if I needed hearing aids or if I was just tired of listening to her and was tuning her out on purpose. Thankfully, the technician saved me. After an extensive test, he revealed that indeed I had lost 25 to 30 percent of my hearing in both ears. He recommended a pair of hearing aids that cost a thousand dollars. When I tried them out, all I could hear was the swooshing noise from my ventilator. I pretty much had to choose either breathing or hearing better, so I immediately opted for breathing. Much to my chagrin, Jo Anne hesitated while she weighed the options, but she finally agreed that breathing was just a little more important than hearing well. I was relieved!

However, I believe hearing well and listening carefully to others are almost as important as breathing. The people I enjoy visiting with the most are those who truly listen to me and seem genuinely interested in what I have to say. When I am in a crowded place like Costco, for example, most people don't pay much attention to me. But on occasion, a random individual will approach me and say, "Wow, what an incredible wheelchair you have. How does it work?" And then they really listen and ask even more questions like, "What happened to you, anyway?" Whenever I have these experiences with strangers, my life is enriched because they validate me as a human being and a person of worth through their desire to hear and listen and understand.

Many years ago I learned a great lesson about the importance of listening. I was teaching a religious class at the Utah State Industrial School in Ogden, Utah, which in reality was a prison for juvenile delinquents who had run awry of the law.

One year I went to the maximum security unit once each day to teach a class to the boys incarcerated there because they were either considered dangerous or a security risk. They wore blue jeans, white T-shirts, and tennis shoes with no laces. These boys were extremely depressed. Several guards watched them twenty-four hours a day from a glass booth strategically positioned so that the kids were never out of earshot or sight.

Almost all the boys attended my class, not because I was a great teacher, but because I didn't work for the state and therefore had no power over them. It was a diversion to have someone like me visit them while they were doing their time in maximum security.

After a simple lesson regarding fundamental principles of life—like working instead of stealing, being honest instead of lying, respecting the sanctity of life, and so on—I would stay another hour to do some individual counseling. The boys

would frantically gather around me at the conclusion of our formal class, saying, "Mr. Rushton, talk to me today. Please talk to me!" I would try to give everyone a fair chance. I quickly learned, however, that what they were really saying was, "*Listen* to me. Please *listen* to me!" I would say little during those counseling sessions, but I would give them my undivided attention. It seemed to help, even though their problems were so overwhelming I doubt that even Solomon could have had the wisdom to help solve them.

In maximum security I learned how important it is to truly be listened to. I got the impression that many of those disturbed young men had never truly been listened to by a significant adult in their lives. Sad to say, many of these young men died violently and prematurely or ended up in the state penitentiary. No, they didn't live happily ever after because I listened to them. But at least for a few hours, somebody truly listened to them. It was a soothing balm for their harrowed up souls, if only for a brief period of time.

Many years later after my accident, I had a similar experience. Jo Anne and I took a trip to Arizona to visit our good friends, the Gardners. Miles and his wife, Barb, accepted the assignment to visit the men and women prisoners who were of their faith. Knowing of our impending visit, they thought it would be a good idea if I could visit with them as well. I accepted, not knowing exactly what I might say to them or how they might even perceive me.

First, we visited the women. It was quite an experience just to get inside the facility. There were many security hoops to jump through. I wondered once we got in if we would be able to get out.

We finally arrived at the appointed room where the women were waiting for us. After an introduction and a brief message that I delivered, we asked if any of the women had questions. Instead of asking questions, they wanted to share their problems and pain. Like those young boys, I knew they just wanted to be listened to. Visiting with the men was very similar. Upon meeting me, many of them were anxious to share their story. I doubt I did any real good. Perhaps I at least made them feel good that they weren't paralyzed. However, I knew the real truth. Although I was a prisoner in my own body, I had more freedom than they ever would.

I think the greatest gift we can give to our family and friends is to truly listen to them and give them our undivided attention. Turning off the TV, looking away from our computer screen, closing a book, or leaving an important unfinished task in order to listen to a loved one will convey love in a way few other things can.

A renowned heart surgeon, Russell M. Nelson, said something wonderful about listening that strikes a chord with me:

A wise father once said, "I do a greater amount of good when I listen to my children than when I talk to them.". . . The time to listen is when someone needs to be heard. . . . Parents with teenage youth may find that time for listening is often less convenient but more important when young people feel lonely or troubled. And when they seem to deserve favor least, they may need it most. . . . Some couples seem not to listen to one another. . . . If marriage is a prime relationship in life, it deserves prime time! Yet less important appointments are often given priority, leaving only leftover moments for listening to precious partners."[1]

Choosing between breathing or listening is a hard call. But just as breathing gives life to the body, listening gives life to all the precious relationships we have in mortality.

When I learned I had lost the use of my physical body, I realized that the only thing that meant anything to me was the relationships I had with my family, my friends, and the Lord. Nothing else I had accomplished in my life—no worldly possession, no degrees or honors of men—meant anything to me. If learning to listen better can strengthen all those relationships, how we ought to work at it!

Are you listening?

Dad / Grandpa / Jack

Note
1. Russell M. Nelson, "Listen to Learn," *Ensign*, May 1991.

The Precious
PRESENT

WHILE WAITING FOR Jo Anne one day, I stared at a picture frame hanging on the dining room wall. Jo Anne had created a collage of pictures of me interacting with members of my family before my accident. I rolled my chair over to the collage so I could see it better. In one of the photos, I had my arm around my oldest son at his high school graduation. In another, I posed with my oldest daughter at her wedding reception. And in another, I held my oldest grandson shortly after his birth.

As I sat there looking at those photographs, I was overcome by a sobering thought: "Jack, you really didn't know how good life was as you were going through it, did you? You took so many things for granted. Remember what it was like to pick up your children in your arms and carry them upstairs, put them to bed, and sing them to sleep. Think of all the basketball games out in the driveway with your sons and the neighborhood kids. What a blessing to

Jack and his oldest daughter, Jo Lene, at her
wedding reception.

be able to sit down at the piano and play or use those same
fingers to work at the computer. Remember how good it
was to be able to get up in the morning and put on your
running shoes, and in that beautiful and peaceful time just
before dawn, to run through the neighborhood, exercising your body and planning out your day. Do you recall
how good it was to be able to hug Jo Anne?" Memories
continued to flood my mind, and I regretted that I had
not valued those experiences as much as I could have at
the time.

As I sat there, I realized how important it is to enjoy the
moment—the precious present—and to not live so much in
the past or in the future. We need to be grateful for the particular season we are experiencing in our lives and not be in

such a hurry to just get through it.

Awhile back we had Dumpster Day in our little community of Tustin Meadows. Large dumpsters are brought in, and on the designated day we can take all our junk and deposit it in one of the dumpsters. As that great day approaches, Jo Anne searches through the house, with a gleam in her eye, looking for anything with no value. Any possession that is not carrying its weight by serving some utilitarian purpose ends up in the dumpster. I became very nervous because she seemed to be spending an inordinate amount of time in my office. Each time she looked at me, I tried to say something intelligent, blink my eyes, and give her my most endearing smile. I did not want to end up in the dumpster with the rest of the stuff gathering dust.

The morning of Dumpster Day, I saw her eyeing the shelf where my journals are kept. Finally, in a panic, I convinced her that they don't eat anything and I would pay rent on the space they occupy if she wouldn't throw them out. She relented, and we ended up reading some interesting journal entries I had made just before I had my accident. The following are my last two entries before being injured.

June 30, 1989 (one month and one day before my accident): *The Lord has blessed me tremendously and my heart is filled with gratitude when I think of the many blessings we enjoy as a family: the new grandchildren, Mike soon to be in law school, Jo Lene managing to teach while enjoying her firstborn, Rich serving in Columbia,*

John in high school learning some things about life and work. The little girls are so precious to me that I can't even express myself regarding them. Life would be so empty without these special people. What can I say about Jo Anne? Life would be no good without her. I love her more now than I did 25 years ago.

July 26, 1989 (five days before the fateful trip to Laguna Beach): *Jo Anne and I celebrated our 25th wedding anniversary last week. . . . It was just special being with her and contemplating the things that have happened in 25 year of marriage. If I had to do it all over again, I wouldn't want to change a thing.*

And then, suddenly, we began a new season of our lives. Although there was a long period of adjustment, this new season of our lives has been remarkably wonderful and fulfilling. It has taught me to enjoy the precious present.

For example, awhile back, Jo Anne and I drove over to her mother's home in Santa Ana. Her dad had passed away several years before, and her mother had joined him the previous summer. The home was up for sale, and Jo Anne wanted to spruce up the plants and shrubs in front of the home. She actually enjoys working in the garden, and I believe she has inherited some of her dad's Idaho farmer genes. In fact, since I have been paralyzed and she oversees the yard care, our lawn has never looked so good.

She said we would only be there about an hour, which translates into three hours—she is severely time challenged. It was a beautiful day, but instead of getting out of the van and sitting in the sun, I opted to remain in the van with the door and windows open. I must admit, I enjoy watching Jo Anne work with a shovel and rake with no guilty conscience on my part, given my physical condition.

Our van's CD player holds six CDs, so I just sat there watching Jo Anne working, listening to great music, and reflecting back on my life. Every once in a while Jo Anne would come by the van, smile, and shrug her shoulders, trying to communicate that she was sorry she was taking so long but had to keep working. She could have saved the smile and the shrug because I was having a most pleasant afternoon. I was feeling a complete sense of peace that is difficult to describe.

I have learned a great lesson, and I try hard to no longer live so much in the past or in the future, but strive to enjoy the precious present. Each day is a gift to be valued. I'm afraid that one of the most frequently committed sins—at least in my life—has been the sin of ingratitude. We take so much for granted so much of the time. I think we must be very careful to always express our appreciation to a loving and kind Heavenly Father through our prayers and our actions. He is the source—the fount—of all of our blessings, both spiritual and material. To recognize this fact daily is perhaps the wisest and most important thing we can do to keep life in proper perspective.

Dad/Grandpa/Jack

Never
GIVE UP!

IN 1945 VICTOR E. Frankl wrote his landmark book, *Man's Search for Meaning*, in which he reflects on living through the Holocaust and witnessing the deaths of his family. I read the book for the first time as a college student, and it had a great impact on me. Now, after many years of being paralyzed from the neck down and on life support, his words are even more profound and meaningful to me.

His insights and reflections on the survivors are timeless and applicable to anyone who has faced seemingly impossible circumstances. Like those who lived in the death camps, many individuals endure great trials—paralysis, cancer, heart problems, multiple sclerosis, marital and family problems, financial problems, and so forth—but react to them in different ways. In the death camps, many simply gave up and died, while others survived and eventually led happy, productive lives. The same is true with the less dramatic trials that so many of us experience. Some simply give up in the face of their adversity, while others, faced with the same adversity, grow stronger and survive the seemingly unsurvivable.

Frankl observed that those who survived the death camps shared a common trait: "A man who becomes conscious of the responsibility he bears toward a human being who affectionately waits for him, or to an unfinished work, will never be able to throw away his life. He knows the 'why' for his existence, and will be able to bear almost any 'how.' "[1]

I believe Frankl was saying that if we know our family members need our love and they love us in return, and if we have a work that we wish to complete, we will be blessed with a desire to live and press forward, regardless of the seemingly impossible odds we are facing.

My nephew John Michael Stuart is a great example of this. I rejoice in the quality of life he has achieved and the quality of person he has become. John was born with cerebral palsy and is in his mid-forties now. His condition is not as severe as others' with the disease, but life has been a struggle for him from the beginning. He walks with great difficulty and is very shaky with his hands and arms. Eating by himself is a challenge. He will grab his right hand with his left hand, and with much effort and concentration, he will try to get the food from his plate into his mouth without dropping it. His speech is somewhat difficult to understand, but if you listen carefully, he is able to communicate effectively.

From him I have learned a great lesson about life that I did not fully appreciate until I had my accident and was bound to a wheelchair. John has become a great example to me as I have seen what he has done with his life. John attended special schools until he was ready to go to high school. He had great hopes of fitting in with the "norm," but it was not easy. He had to work harder than anybody else, but he eventually graduated. Lest you think he is slow, nothing could be further from the truth. Although trapped in a body that won't work for him, he has an indomitable spirit and a great intellect.

Not content to use his disability as an excuse and adopt a life of leisure, he graduated from college with a bachelor's degree in political science. Then, to my surprise, he went on to get a master's degree in social work. I found it very ironic that somebody in John's physical situation would choose a vocation involving helping people with problems.

After receiving his masters degree, John was hired by a large HMO as a social worker. His clients loved him for his integrity, hard work ethic, and empathy for them and their problems, which oftentimes were not as challenging as his own.

John is bright beyond bright, has read widely and deeply, is a motivational speaker, and has written a book about how life's adversities can make us stronger.

In his book, *The Perfect Circle*, he shares his experience with one of his professors, who was the chairperson of the social work department. Up to this point, John had invested over two and one half years toward his degree. She called him into her office and in a heartfelt way told him that he would

John M. Stuart

never be able to make it in social work because no one would ever give credibility to someone who had a disability. She proceeded to inform him that no social service agency would even be willing to hire him.

By this time, however, John had already interned at a rehabilitation hospital and had successfully interacted with patients and their families. He had received a nearly perfect score on an internship evaluation from the supervisor who had observed his professional abilities. John writes, "Yes, there were those who told me I couldn't go to college, much less get my Masters, and there I was doing it. By not allowing others to place their preconceived limitations on me, not only would I be able to be a social worker, I would be, in reality, a great one, disability and all."

Other factors that influence survival are faith and hope. Several weeks ago Jo Anne had me watch a documentary about people with remarkable survival stories. Many of these people were severely injured and should have died, but did not. One man lost both legs when a train ran over him. He should have died on the spot, but he was able to keep his wits and call for help on his cell phone. He continues to live a productive life without legs.

The moderator had interviewed dozens of survivors

all over the world and discovered a common element in all those who had the will to live and did so: faith in God. The survivors were all from different religious traditions, but they believed that God could help them, and their faith gave them the hope and the will to cling to life.

Coupled with love and support from our families, and daily goals to accomplish good, faith and hope will kindle within our hearts the will to live and be productive. How proud I am of the many individuals I know who are battling cancer with great courage or have other difficult health challenges. They fight valiantly, never giving up, and bless so many lives in the process.

One of my favorite historical figures is Winston Churchill. The essence of his life is captured in the words he spoke to his countrymen during the dark days of World War II: "NEVER, NEVER, NEVER GIVE UP!" I hope his words will be the essence of our lives, regardless of what circumstances life may bring our way.

Dad/Grandpa/Jack

Notes
1. Victor Frankl, *Man's Search for Meaning*, 127.

Faith—Beyond
ENDURING

Enduring It
WELL

ONE FALL AFTERNOON, I was sitting in my bedroom with several of my friends, watching a college football game on my 47-inch flat screen TV. Jo Anne had made homemade pizza, which we were devouring with enormous amounts of root beer, candy, nuts, and brownies. We were all so happy with the way the game was going. Almost imperceptibly, the momentum switched to the other team. After all that pizza, we felt a growing sense of doom and the need for a big shot of Alka-Seltzer or a mega dose of aspirin.

Sure enough, our team gave the game away to their guest, 50–51. My friends suddenly disappeared, and I found myself alone in my now not-so-cheerful bedroom. Jo Anne came in to clean up the leftover food and wondered how the game had turned out. I told her the score and she said, "Isn't that an awful lot of home runs in one football game?" I assured her it was.

I believe one of the virtues of sports is that it teaches us the importance of enduring well to the end. If we don't endure well to the end of our lives, then even scoring fifty points in a football game, so to speak (even though it is an "awful lot of home runs"), ultimately won't do us much good.

On another occasion, Jo Anne hosted a bridal shower at our home. One of the ladies who attended brought her son to visit with me during the shower. It was such a great blessing to be cloistered away in my bedroom with some male companionship and protected from the girlish chatter that forty women inevitably bring with them to a bridal shower. I was not reluctant, however, to partake of the good food and dessert.

The young man I was privileged to visit with was badly injured while riding his bicycle. His pancreas was severely damaged, and his life had been in jeopardy for some time. For months he was unable to eat and as a result lost over fifty pounds. After many prayers on his behalf and skilled doctors performing a delicate surgery, he was beginning to eat again and was regaining his health and strength. If everything keeps going well, he should function normally in another six months.

He is a wonderful person with great potential and promise. He was attending USC on an academic scholarship before the accident. What has happened to him, I am sure, has caused him much serious reflection.

He asked me many questions that day, and I truly had a delightful time visiting with him. Toward the end of our conversation, he asked what I thought was a question for the ages: "What do you think I should learn from this experience?"

It seems like such a simple question, yet it is very profound. Because he asked this question, I knew he had been doing a lot of soul-searching as to why he had to experience this kind of problem. What follows is in essence what I tried to share with him that evening, but in more detail as I have had time to reflect on it for a few days.

The first thing that came into my mind was that hopefully he would learn patience. However, I really mean much more than just patience. The scriptures would call it learning to endure. But it is also more than just doing that. When my own accident occurred, I was fifty years old, had been married twenty-five years, had a good family, and had a wonderful career in teaching. With all that experience behind me, I felt that I was strong enough to handle what had happened to me.

In my mind I said, "Jack, you can get through this. It won't be easy, but you can do it. Just gird up your loins and gut it out." And so, like a man in a cold wind and rain storm, I turned up the collar of my coat, turned my back to the storm, gritted my teeth, and endured. Guess what? It didn't work!

I was miserable, and my family was miserable. Eventually, through sincere prayer and scripture study, I began to understand that just enduring was not enough. I needed to endure it well. I realized that there was still much I could do and that I would be held accountable for not using my gift of life to do more than just exist and survive. I knew that because of my physical condition, all I could really do was use my mind and my voice. As I started doing so, it paved the way for a much happier way of life. It was amazing to me how much better my relationship with Jo Anne became because I began to be much more open in sharing things with her. My children and grandchildren even responded to me more positively as I began reaching out to them more.

I now see each day as a day of challenge and hope. What can I do today to be productive? To whom can I write? What can I read that will enable me to gain wisdom and understanding of life and of eternal life? Although physically I can't do anything, my mind and spirit are intact, and I can still do everything that really matters. The change may not be visible to those outside the family, but the change is real and I feel it deep inside.

You are probably saying, "Well, Jack, that is all well and good, but how do you get to that point in your life where, in they immediately saw that except for not being able to walk, he was the same wonderful person he had been before. He said, "Before my injury I could do a thousand things. Now I can only do five hundred. However, I am not eating out my heart because of the five hundred things I can't do but am grateful for the five hundred I can do."

With my reduced ability to see, I can no longer read the printed word and therefore cannot use notes when speaking or teaching. Therefore, I have forced myself to memorize the most important things I want to say. Sometimes, however, I feel that I am just about one step away from being brain dead as I try to memorize something. I have learned that it is easier for me to memorize scripture than anything else. In doing so I have found that the verses take on added meaning when they are memorized—they become part of me—and when delivered as part of a talk for church, they seem to take on added power. I find that as I memorize a talk, I have great freedom when I finally deliberate. Having it in my mind and in my heart, I seem to be more open to inspiration for additional ideas that come to me at the moment of delivery.

With my diminished eyesight, I have a much greater empathy for those who are blind than I ever had before. With my "long distance" glasses I can watch TV pretty well and can enjoy going outside, but I can't see well enough to read the street signs. Actually, this has been a blessing as Jo Anne drives me about. I have lost the sense of impending doom that used to accompany me on most of our journeys. I

the midst of adversity, you are able to rise to a level beyond just enduring—to enduring it well?"

After my accident, I often asked myself, "Why are terrible things that happen to us supposed to be for our good?" I just didn't get it! Yes, I knew they give us experience, but was that all? Was being paralyzed from the neck down and living on life support the rest of my life for my good? Was it for the good of this young man to almost lose his life in a bicycle accident? Finally, after much pondering, I finally understood.

All of the horrible things that can happen to us in mortality will only be for our good if they humble us, drive us to our knees, and make us more dependent upon the Savior and less dependent upon worldly things. Adversity can either drive people away from their faith in Christ or to an increased faith in Him. When a person comes to understand that he is not strong enough or smart enough to make it on his own and comes to Christ, then Christ strengthens him to endure it well. Only then will the adversity be for his good.

And so, my young friend, hopefully you will learn to endure it well and turn to the Lord, casting your burden upon Him with complete trust and faith in His goodness. If you do so, I believe I can promise you, because of my own experience, you will always be able to rejoice and be filled with the love of God, regardless of what life may bring your way.

Dad/Grandpa/Jack

OBSERVATION TWENTY-FIVE

I Don't Look
SO GOOD

AN OLD FARMER wanted to sell one of his horses, so he ran an ad in the local newspaper which in part said, "The horse doesn't look so good." A few days after the ad appeared, a man drove out to his farm to examine the horse. The horse was gorgeous, and the price was more than right, so he bought it, thinking he had really put one over on the old farmer. Two days later, he was back at the farm with his recent purchase. He said to the farmer, "Why didn't you tell me the horse was blind?" The farmer smiled weakly as he responded, "I said he didn't look so good!"

I'm afraid I am like that old horse. After a number of unsuccessful retinal surgeries, I have lost my sight in one eye and don't look so good out of the other one. I have now had two retinal surgeries on my good eye. The first one did not successfully attach the retina, but the second one did, and things seem to be progressing well. During this second procedure, they removed

all the fluid from my eye, and using a laser, the doctor welded the retina in place and then filled it with oil. I recommended that he use 20/20 Pennzoil, but instead he filled it with special silicone oil that is standard operating procedure for this kind of surgery. Although the retina is attached, my vision is somewhat distorted because of the oil. Perhaps I can opt for an oil change sometime down the road. However, I'm grateful that I can see well enough to not be considered blind. With very powerful reading glasses, sitting as close as I can to my computer monitor and using large fonts, I am able to read and write.

Everything in life is relative. When I was first injured, I didn't think things could get much worse. I didn't even think about what a blessing it was to have almost perfect vision and hearing. Now I don't think about being paralyzed, but I have spent some time considering what a priceless gift sight is. Having essentially lost the ability to see out of my right eye and now having impaired vision in my left eye, I almost asked, "Why me, Lord?" Thankfully I never got that low and instead, miraculously, began to feel grateful for what vision I still have.

My situation reminds me of the story of a great young man who was left a paraplegic after a serious car accident. His friends hesitated to visit him because they just couldn't imagine what he would be like now. Previously he had been dynamic, enthusiastic, and happy, so when they visited, they dragged their feet all the way to his door, not knowing what to expect. He opened the door and as he greeted

suppose I will only realize how dangerous things have really become when it is too late to do anything about it.

Not having been able to read or write while my eye was healing caused me to do more pondering and reflecting than usual. For some reason, almost every evening or morning while I was in bed a scripture from the Gospel of John that has been set to music constantly played in my mind. One of the things I miss most about my current situation is my ability to sing. I sang in many choirs and even directed them. For some reason every choir I conducted or sang in always learned and performed the following: "Peace I leave with you, my peace I give unto you: not as the world giveth, give I unto you. Let not your heart be troubled, neither let it be afraid" (John 14:27).

I can never just recite these words. I almost involuntarily sing them in my mind. And so, for some months, without consciously striving to do so, these words and melody were almost constantly in my mind. I am kind of dense, but I began to think the Lord was addressing the fact that my heart was somewhat troubled and afraid regarding the possibility of impending blindness. I believe that was undoubtedly part of it, which was sure evidence of a lack of faith in Christ and the power of the Atonement. However, that was just part of the message the Lord wanted me to receive as I pondered the words of the Savior recorded by John.

The verse begins, "Peace I leave with you." Yes, Christ was the Prince of Peace and was not the great warrior the Jews expected to free them from the yoke of Roman bondage. He left the world in peace in the sense that no armed conflict erupted or was inspired by Him during His ministry. That was important, but then He goes to the heart of that matter—something I needed to understand: "My peace I give unto you; not as the world giveth, give I unto you." Now he talks about another kind of peace—*my peace*! And He doesn't just *leave* it with us. He *gives* it to us. The gift of His peace enables us to never let our hearts be troubled or afraid. If we seek Him and trust in His goodness, He will give us *His* peace—not as the world giveth.

His peace is spiritual in nature and hard to describe to one who has never felt it. Paul said it passes all human understanding. And it does. But it is real. The peace the world offers comes from important institutions of men such as stable governments, law and order, and the United Nations. Unfortunately, the world's peace seems to be enforced by weapons of destruction—quite an ironic paradox.

I have greatly needed this message from John 14:27 at this time in my life. Thankfully, trouble and fear have been replaced by the peace that only the Savior can bring into one's heart. The Savior's gift of peace is priceless!

Each morning when I see the sunshine peeking around the edges of the blinds in my bedroom, I am so grateful I can see. I know I have been given another day in which I can see the faces of those I love, read and write on the computer, observe this beautiful world, and even watch a Lakers game.

Dad/Grandpa/Jack

DELIVERANCE

LAST WEEK JO ANNE and I had a bittersweet experience. Our son Richard lives nearby, and one of his neighbors is an occupational therapist who works at a little care facility in Tustin. She knows about our situation and has seen our DVD, *It's Good to Be Alive*. She called Jo Anne and asked her if she could bring two young quadriplegics to our home to visit with us.

The quadriplegics were young Mexicans in their late twenties or early thirties. Both had fallen off roofs while doing construction and suffered severe spinal cord injuries. Thankfully, they are not on life support and can move their arms about, but they can't use their fingers, which makes them quadriplegics as defined by the medical community.

Although we could sense that José and Leo had sweet spirits, they were depressed and subdued. José has a wife and four children who live in Mexico. I don't believe he has seen them since his accident, and now because of his injury, he has no way of supporting them or bringing them to the United States. His situation seems very hopeless to him.

Leo also feels hopeless about his situation. His wife and three children rent a small house in a community near our home. Although he has been home a few times and his wife and children visit him at the facility when they can, he still feels depressed about the situation. He can't go home to live with them because the house is not wheelchair accessible. And even if he had the money, he couldn't modify the house because it is a rental.

The occupational therapist brought them to our home to help them enlarge their vision and gain hope that there is life after paralysis. Thankfully I was able to communicate with them in Spanish—they barely spoke English—and we connected and had a good experience together. They were impressed with what I could do on the computer and with what Jo Anne does to make our lives fulfilling. I wish I had the power to deliver them from their dark and depressing situations, but I believe they left with a small glimmer of hope in their eyes.

Their visit reminded me of the six months I spent at Rancho Los Amigos Rehabilitation Hospital in the spinal cord injury unit. I was roommates with Gene Nye, who was twenty-one years old at the time. I used to talk a lot about Gene in speeches I would give to different groups and the valuable lessons I learned from him during that time.

Gene worked for the forest service in the mountains. One day he was bitten or infected by a wild animal and was severely stricken by spinal meningitis. The high fever damaged his brain, and when I met him, his body and face were contorted, he was partially paralyzed, he couldn't breathe on his own, and he couldn't think straight or speak.

Gene's situation seemed incredibly hopeless to me because he not only had staggering physical challenges, but he was also an orphan. During the six months we were together, he only had two visitors; two men he used to work with came by one afternoon to say hello. How I wanted to deliver Gene from his miserable lot in life!

These three men are only a few of the examples of the countless people who are dealing with seemingly hopeless situations and have become depressed, lonely, and miserable. Is there no deliverance for them from this sorrow and heartache? The answer, of course, is yes. However, their deliverance will not come to them through the arm of flesh, but through the great Deliverer.

My daughter Rachel was only nine years old at the time of my accident. She and my youngest daughter, Jackie, have grown up helping their mother bathe, dress, and feed me as well as help transfer me from my bed to the wheelchair and vice versa. As Rachel got older, she often put me to bed by herself. I think helping me gave her the desire to become a nurse.

Upon Rachel's graduation, I got to meet Dr. Elaine S. Marshall, the dean of her College of Nursing. Prior to meeting her, I had read an article she had written that had a great impact on me. It was titled "Lessons on Healing." She put

into words something that I had felt to be true for years but had never been able to fully express.

She believes that there is a big difference between being cured and being healed. She wrote, "Cure is clean, quick, and done, often under anesthesia. Healing, however, is often a lifetime process of recovery and growth in spite of—or perhaps because of—enduring physical, emotional, or spiritual assault. It often requires time. We may pray for cure when we really need healing."[1]

In her article she indicated that she had studied the four Gospels to discover what she could about Jesus as a healer. I love Elaine Marshall's summary from the scriptures of this aspect of the Savior's ministry.

> As Jesus healed, the Scriptures say, All the people were amazed (Matthew 12:23). They brought their sick, their blind, and dumb, those that were possessed by a devil (Matthew 12:22), and their dead. They sought

him every day and into the evening. So great was his reputation and his healing power that they sought to only touch the hem of his garment; and as many as touched were made perfectly whole (Matthew 14:36). And Jesus went about all the cities and villages, teaching . . . and preaching the gospel . . . and healing every sickness and every disease among the people (Matthew 9:35).[2]

The Savior is the master healer of the soul—both body and spirit. In retrospect, I believe I was cured from my injury as far as medical science was concerned within a year after the accident. If you were to read my medical chart, it would say something like this: "Jack Rushton is a functioning quadriplegic on life support having sustained a complete injury between the second and third cervical vertebrae."

I may have been cured as far as medicine could cure me, but I was a long way from being healed. I was still devastated and felt that so much had been taken away from me. I was depressed and had little hope of what the future might bring. Many years ago, after much soul searching and intense prayer, a wonderful thing happened. The Lord saw fit to heal me as only He can. He gave me a new heart. Since then, I have felt joy and a sense of well-being that I never thought I would feel again.

Many of us never receive the total physical cure we desire. However, this must not stop us from seeking to be healed. When we seek the Lord with all our heart, He can strengthen us to the point that our burdens will seem light and bearable.

From the beginning of time, God has tried to teach his people that if they will but trust in Him, He will deliver them from captivity, bondage, and seemingly hopeless circumstances.

And so I would like to say to Leo, Jose, Gene, and countless others, there is no deliverance except through Christ. Christ can infuse joy into our souls and dispel the cloud of darkness hanging over us as nothing else can. No man can do it for us; no other human being can deliver us from sorrow and despair, except the Great Deliverer.

Dad / Grandpa / Jack

Notes
1. Elaine S. Marshall, "Lessons on Healing," *Ensign*, Apr. 2004, 57.
2. Ibid.

Good Luck,
BAD LUCK

ONE DAY A Chinese farmer's horse escaped into the hills. When the farmer's neighbors sympathized with him over his bad luck, he replied, "Bad luck? Good luck? Who knows?" A week later, the horse returned with a herd of horses from the hills, and this time the neighbors congratulated the farmer on his good luck. His reply was, "Good luck? Bad luck? Who knows?"

When the farmer's son was taming one of the wild horses, he fell off its back and broke his leg. Everyone thought this was very bad luck, except the farmer, whose only reaction was, "Bad luck? Good luck? Who knows?"

Some weeks later, the army marched into the village and conscripted every able-bodied youth they found. When they discovered the farmer's son had broken a leg, they let him go. Was that good luck or bad luck? Who knows?

The old Chinese farmer had a sage philosophy on life. It is difficult to accurately judge whether the things that happen to us are good luck or bad luck. Usually only the passage of time will reveal how good or how bad a particular situation has actually been.

Some time ago, Jo Anne, her sister Janice, and I drove to St. George, Utah, to attend a funeral. At one point we pulled off the freeway to get something to eat. As is normally the case with us, the keys were lost. Bad luck. In Spanish the use of reflexive verbs lets everyone off the hook in most cases, and so as it would be said in Spanish, "The keys lost themselves." Jo Anne and Janice were frantically looking everywhere while I was contributing advice that for some reason seemed not to be overly appreciated. An hour later they found the keys in a crevice in a corner of the back seat. Good luck. I refuse to disclose how many hours it took us to arrive at our destination. Bad luck.

Jo Anne's brother, John, and his wife, Alex, had a foster son, David. David was born with spina bifida and given away by his mother at a very young age. Bad luck. John and Alex met David when he was a young boy through the school that their own son, John Michael, born with cerebral palsy, was attending at the time. Not one couple in thousands would have taken David into their home with all of his physical and emotional problems. But John and Alex did so and proved to be the greatest blessing that ever came into David's life. Good luck.

About a month after my accident while I was at Rancho Los Amigos Rehabilitation Hospital, one afternoon David and Rod Scrivner, his friend with spina bifida, came wheeling into my room. These two boys wanted to let me know that I could have a decent quality of life even in a wheelchair. They visited for some time, and I am sure they felt very comfortable in that vast spinal cord injury unit at Rancho. I always remembered that kind visit from David, and from that time on, he would seek me out at family gatherings so we could talk. He saw me as someone who could identify with his situation, and our conversations were always open

David

regarding common problems and challenges we faced because of our physical circumstances.

I could only identify with David, however, up to a point. I had fifty good years of "normal" life before becoming a quadriplegic on life support. I had been blessed with a wonderful wife and family. My life had been productive and fulfilling in every way prior to my accident. I didn't know what it was like to be born with spina bifida, rejected by my mother, and experience countless operations and health problems all my life. I don't think anyone totally understood or knew what David had experienced in forty-one years of life except one person—the Savior.

He understood David and what he was experiencing. The Savior knew how to help and bless David as nobody else could. Because of that he brought John and Alex into David's life, knowing that this couple had what it took to be an extension of His love to bless this abandoned and physically challenged little boy.

The night of the Last Supper, the Savior made a significant promise to his apostles that applies to all of us as well: "I will not leave you comfortless: I will come to you" (John 14:18). A better translation from the original Greek would have been, "I will not leave you orphans." We are His beloved children, spiritually begotten sons and daughters through the Atonement, and He will come to us in our unique and individual circumstances. He will never leave us "orphans."

I believe He comes to us in a variety of ways. Certainly, He manifests His love for us and brings us comfort through the gift of the Holy Ghost. I also believe He comes to us in the form of other people who frequently, not knowing they are being guided by Him, become an extension and manifestation of His pure love. I believe such was the case with David. John and Alex were an extension and manifestation of Christ's love for David.

Christ's love for me in my paralysis has been manifested not only through the Comforter, but in the form of Jo Anne, my children, and many dear friends. In some way that I do not even begin to pretend to understand, the Savior knows what it is like to be paralyzed and living on life support. He intimately knows each one of us and our unique challenges. He will not leave us "orphans" if we have faith and absolute trust in Him.

When I had my accident, my family couldn't help but think it was bad luck. Nothing like this had ever happened to us, and the thought of me being paralyzed from the neck down and on life support the rest of my life was almost more than we could bear. We could not see any good luck in it or why God would allow this to happen to me. Years later, we still probably do not have all the answers, but I now believe that much good has come from what once seemed so bad.

There is no way I could ever express verbally what I have learned about the power of the Atonement through my experience with paralysis. I have also learned things about myself and been strengthened in ways that perhaps would not have been possible without this challenging experience. I will always believe that my younger two daughters have been blessed with a level of spirituality that may not have been theirs had they not had so much responsibility thrust upon them at such tender ages. I have also witnessed Jo Anne shoulder a monumental responsibility and grow spiritually and emotionally.

One of the things we need most in life—and often must struggle to obtain—is an eternal vision accompanied by complete trust and faith in the ultimate goodness of God, His love for us, and His desire to bless each of us.

So you really won the lottery? Good luck? Bad luck? Who knows?

Dad/Grandpa/Jack

CONTENTMENT

THE OTHER DAY I was talking to a good friend of mine on the telephone. He is a few years older than me and for a number of years has been battling a lung condition that makes it hard for him to breathe. His body has also weakened, and it is hard for him to get around. He was telling me about the little electric cart he loads into the back of his pickup truck using a special device that has been invented for just that purpose. He is then able to drive around the malls and other stores he enjoys visiting, like Home Depot. His home sits on a fairly large lot with plenty of grass. He told me about the wonderful lawn mower he had just purchased that enables him to drive about to keep his lawn manicured, and how much he enjoys doing it.

I then shared with him how much I enjoy my laptop computer and the voice recognition software that allows me to be creative and productive. I also told him that my eyesight is not very good, and I enjoy my 42-inch high-definition TV. By sitting as close to it as I can, I can see almost perfectly. What a joy!

We continued to share the things we were able to do. Then he said, "For as bad off as we are, we have it pretty good." He was absolutely right!

It is a great blessing to be content, at peace, and happy, regardless of what life may bring our way. The Apostle Paul is the perfect example of this. He spent years in dungeons, came close to death on many occasions, was shipwrecked three times, was stoned and whipped and beaten, and suffered much hunger and cold. He also wrote that he had a "thorn in the flesh," some ailment from which he was never cured (2 Corinthians 11:23-28; 12:7–8). Despite his many afflictions, he still said, "I have learned in whatsoever state I am therewith to be content" (Philippians 4:11). But how could he be content in such dire circumstances? In verse 13 he said, "I can do all things through Christ who strengtheneth me." Paul teaches us that regardless of what life brings us, with the help of God, we can find peace, joy, and even contentment in our individual circumstances.

However, a wise man cautioned that even though we should be content with our circumstances, we should not be content with ourselves. He said, "We can and ought to be content with the things allotted to us, being circumstantially content but without being self-satisfied and behaviorally content with ourselves."[1]

Each of us will face circumstances that we have little or no control over. When these circumstances come, we must accept them and learn to be content with them. However, we should never fall into the trap of letting our circumstances limit our behavior or keep us from achieving our true potential. Paul's life is a great example of this truth.

Many years ago, I took a graduate sociology class at USC. The only thing I remember about the class is the concept of relative deprivation, which I knew to be true the moment I heard it. The concept is simple. Any deprivation we may feel in life is only relative to that to which we have been exposed. Upon discovering this concept, my mind immediately turned to my experience in the western highlands of Guatemala as a twenty-year-old.

I spent approximately one year and a half among the Cachiquel Indians, living in the little villages of Chimaltenango, Patzicia, Tecpan, and Patzun. Their level of poverty was crushing, as was the ever present specter of infant mortality. They grew corn and subsisted for many months of each year solely on corn tortillas. They even burned the tortillas to make a hot drink that tasted as bad as it sounds. When visiting with them after dark in their little adobe, one-room homes, with thatched roofs and dirt floors, we always brought with us our own candles. They couldn't afford candles, and when the sun went down, they simply went to bed. When we left each home, we made sure they had a candle. It was a wonderful gift as far as they were concerned.

Although the people in these villages were not that far from Guatemala City, many of them, especially the women, had never traveled farther than to one or two of the adjacent villages. All they knew about life was what they experienced in the highlands among their own families and friends.

What is the point of this story? These people were happy! They had faith in God. They loved their families and spent time doing the most important things in life. They worked together, played together, worshipped together, and were content in their little corner of the world.

As a young North American coming from the United States, did my companions and I suffer "relative deprivation" upon arriving in and becoming part of this society? In the beginning, we suffered incredibly from this disease until many of the luxuries to which we had grown accustomed faded into the distant recesses of our memories.

After I returned home, it took several years before I could tolerate the affluent society I had grown up in. The longer I was away from Guatemala, however, the more the memory of my wonderful Cachiquel friends faded, and I became once again a participant in affluence.

A number of years ago, I had to spend a great deal of time in bed recovering from a bad pressure sore. One evening Jo Anne and my youngest daughter got me out of bed and into my wheelchair. I rolled outside to the front of the house with my ball cap on and my sandals that looked like new even though they were ten years old. (I wonder why.) It

With Granddaughters Halley and Corallee Brown (ages two and six months).

was a gorgeous evening, nice and warm, with the sun at such an angle that it made everything sparkle and glow. Jo Anne was working in her little flower garden—I love to watch her work—and to me the flowers seemed more beautiful and larger than ever before. I was so happy to be outside in my wheelchair, feeling warm both inside and outside. It felt good to be out of bed with the promise that within an hour or so we would go to In-N-Out Burger for dinner. I can't remember feeling so good, so happy, and so much at peace.

The thought occurred to me that if someone who didn't know me were to walk down the street and see me paralyzed and on life support, wearing dumb sandals and a ball cap, he may have been tempted to mutter to himself, "There but for the grace of God, go I!"

I was reminded of a passage from Victor Frankl's wonderful book, *Man's Search for Meaning*. Describing the horrific conditions in German concentration camps, Frankl related how every possible thing was taken from the Jewish prisoners and how immense their suffering was. Then he made a beautiful and true statement. Having lost everything, the inmates came to understand how "a very trifling thing can cause the greatest of joys."[2]

In my case, being a prisoner in my own body, no one but me knows how the most simple and seemingly "trifling" things are such a source of joy. For me, it is absolutely wonderful to be in my wheelchair, rolling around and having some freedom of movement, even if it's limited.

We must be careful in judging another's suffering or joy. To do so accurately, we would have to have the power to look into the innermost recesses of each person's heart. Lucky is the man or woman who can be content and experience great joy through trifling things.

Dad / Grandpa / Jack

Notes

1. Neal A. Maxwell, "Content with the Things Allotted unto Us," *Ensign*, May 2000, 72.
2. Victor Frankl, *Man's Search for Meaning*, 61–62.

Did God Bring
THE WAVE?

SOME TIME AGO I received a phone call from my son-in-law, Matt Riley, who was enrolled in the MBA program at UC Irvine. The dean had just announced that one of their classmates, Michael Johnson, had drowned in a swimming accident in Northern California the day before. Michael was one of the brightest students and leaders in Matt's MBA class. He was charismatic and had a bright future as a leader in the business world. His fellow classmates were stunned when they received the news. After conferring with the dean and several classmates, Matt volunteered me to speak to about fifty students and offer a prayer of comfort.

Matt came home a few minutes later and drove me up to the campus in our van. As we went into the room where the students were gathered, I could feel the spirit of sorrow, and I could sense that many were asking themselves, "Why did something like this happen to such a good, wonderful person like Michael Johnson?"

Matt had told me, and I could see when I looked at the students, that they were a mix of many races and of a wide variety of religious persuasions, from Matt, a Latter-day Saint, to an avowed atheist. The moment Matt called me, I had started praying for inspiration to know what to say to these young people during such a traumatic time.

I felt strongly impressed to share with them the conversation I had with Dennis Praeger many years ago when I appeared on his talk radio show in Los Angeles called *Religion on the Line*. Toward the end of the hour, Dennis said, "Jack, what brings you the most peace and comfort—to believe that God brought the wave that broke your neck, or to believe that it was just an accident?" In essence, I told him that I had spent very little time asking myself why the accident took place. The only thing I knew for sure was that there was a loving and kind God who would help us get through anything life would bring our way if we had sufficient faith and trust in Him.

I told the students that each of us has our agency and that we are not puppets of deity. Although we exercise our agency and make our own choices, natural law is also at play. Oftentimes in exercising our agency, we hit natural law head on and then must suffer the consequences for our actions.

I chose to go body surfing at Laguna Beach that beautiful August day. I firmly believe that a loving Heavenly Father could have protected me, but He doesn't usually interfere with our agency and natural law. The worst question we could ask ourselves when something like that happens is,

"Why?" God could prevent every disaster or catastrophe from happening, but He doesn't because of His love for us and His understanding of the importance of agency. And so things happen like swimming accidents, cancer, tsunamis, and so on—the list is endless. God doesn't cause these disasters. He could certainly prevent them, but in so doing we would lose the priceless gift of agency.

The students seemed to respond to this line of reasoning, and then I offered a brief prayer of comfort for them and the Michael Johnson family. All of this took no more than five or ten minutes, and then the meeting was opened to the students to express themselves as they desired. Five or six students stood and expressed their feelings about Michael and his accident. Their sorrow was real and palpable. I hope my being there was helpful to some.

Life is so precious, and yet it can be taken in an instant. I am impressed that in our society the preservation of life is a high priority. Every day in the news we hear of thousands of people trying to recover a lost or kidnapped child. If someone is injured in a car accident or stranded on a cliff, many caring people are willing to risk their lives to save the life of another. I believe that medical science, under the inspiration of the Lord, can do much to preserve and improve the quality of human life. When our lives are extended, we can be prepared to take the next step in learning the lessons our individual journeys have to teach us.

Many years ago, a man recognized me and asked, "Are you Jack Rushton?" I told him I was, and he told me he was a doctor at the hospital where I had been taken after my accident. He went to work that night just after I had been transported to the Mission Viejo Trauma Center. He said that the doctors and nurses who had saved my life were standing around talking about what had happened. They were expressing how happy they were that they had been able to save my life, and then one nurse said, "Yes, but did we do him a favor? Maybe it would have been a kinder thing for him to have died than to live his life paralyzed from the neck down and on life support."

The doctor told me that he could hardly wait to go back to the hospital and tell all of those involved in saving my life that he had seen me and that I appeared to be happy and doing well. I told him to please thank them for me and to tell them they truly had done the greatest thing that one human being can do for another in preserving my life.

The last time I saw my dad alive was right before he had open heart surgery to replace a bad valve when he was sixty-one years old. He had some premonitions he might not make it out of the surgery alive, and his last words to me were, "Jake, I ain't been no angel!"

I knew, however, that this was not true. He certainly wasn't perfect, as none of us are, but he had been a wonderful father and had a great love for people and the Lord. I suppose any of us might be tempted to say the same thing under similar circumstances as we evaluate our life. During the past twenty years, I have had many opportunities to leave mortality, but each time I have been rejected. I am not unhappy about that, but I don't care for the idea that I might be considered by the Lord as a "reject." I'm still here, so I guess "I ain't no angel" either.

We cannot put a price on mortal life. Each day is precious and priceless. Even with all my knowledge and faith in life after death, I too am sorry that life was taken unexpectedly from Michael Johnson and my father. I don't believe it was the Lord's will that Michael be taken, but that it was purely and simply a tragic accident, or in my dad's case, a diseased heart. I believe that God wants all of His children to have a long and productive life. However, with the priceless gift of agency and natural law working as it does, accidents occur, and on occasion life is taken prematurely. At times like these our faith in Christ and the promise of a glorious resurrection strengthen us and give us the power to go forward.

Dad / Grandpa / Jack

LUCKY MAN

I HAVE NOTICED over the years that when the Mega Million Lottery reaches over $200 million and nobody wins it, people get a little crazy. The local TV news will show lines of people outside their neighborhood liquor stores, impatiently waiting to buy fistfuls of lottery tickets with their hard-earned money in the hopes they will be lucky enough to strike it rich. The odds of winning the lottery are one in millions, but hope springs eternal.

As I was watching the news the other day, the onsite reporter was interviewing some of the folks in line and asking them what they would do with the money if they were to win the jackpot. I thought one fellow in particular represented many of those in line with his response. He basically said that if he were lucky enough to win the lottery, he would party for two weeks, quit his job, buy homes and cars, and a beautiful, luxurious yacht so he could cruise through life living happily ever after.

The thought occurred to me, "Would one be truly lucky to win the lottery? Would one be lucky to have all the money in the world and live on easy street forever?" You can probably guess what I think.

I looked up the word *lucky* in the Merriam-Webster online dictionary and found several definitions. One was, "Lucky stresses the agency of chance when bringing about a favorable result." However, the synonym I found so meaningful was *providential*, which means "meeting with unforeseen success, but more definitely implies the help or intervention of a higher power."

I think the lottery mentality is aptly described by the first definition of *lucky*. In other words, it is strictly by chance that someone will win mega millions and live happily ever after. Let me explain why the *providential* definition appeals to me.

Following my accident, I spent two weeks in the ICU at the Regional Trauma Center. I was then transferred to a rehabilitation hospital, which became my home for the next six months. As I was rolled on a gurney to the back of the ambulance, a nurse pumped air into my lungs with a handheld ambu bag. The device looks like a football, and one end is attached to the tracheostomy tube that has been surgically placed in one's throat as an airway to the lungs. It is used when one is not attached to the ventilator or if the ventilator should fail. As I lay there, unable to speak or move any part of my body while air was hand pumped into my lungs, another nurse who had spent a great deal of time caring for me looked at Jo Anne and said, "Mrs. Rushton, your husband is a lucky man." As Jo Anne looked at her in disbelief, she continued, "You don't understand what I'm saying just now, but your husband is a lucky man because he will get to experience a part of life that very few do, and he will be a better man because of it."

Although neither of us understood the nurse at the time, her words proved to be prophetic. I actually am a lucky man. I have met with unforeseen success and joy and have experienced God intervening to preserve my life on a number of occasions. I can honestly say, "It's good to be alive!"

In retrospect, it has been quite an adventure and learning experience over the past twenty years.

Dr. Arnold Beisser in his wonderful book, *Flying without Wings*, captured the essence of how I feel at this time in my life. Dr. Beisser contracted polio as a young adult and lived the remainder of his life in a wheelchair, working as a practicing psychiatrist. He said, "My disability has taught me a lot and continues to do so. When I was young and physically strong, to live life from a wheelchair was unthinkable. When I was disabled it was unacceptable. Gradually over the years, however, not only has it become acceptable but I have found it to be satisfying as well."[1]

Before my accident, I felt I had a pretty good idea of who I was, but after the accident I was a little shaky for some time regarding that subject. Quite frankly, for an extended period, I really didn't know who or what I was. It was devastating!

In some ways I felt I had left the human race that I had been part of all my life. Something inside me, however, rebelled against the idea of being labeled as something that I then perceived as being inferior compared to a "normal" person.

Many years ago, before my accident, I spent several summers with some other teachers working at a day camp called Camp Sheanee (an Indian name for "summer people") to earn some extra income. We were given old Volkswagen vans, and each weekday morning we would drive through the beautiful neighborhood streets of San Marino, California, picking up rich kids that we would then entertain all day. At the end of each day, before dropping them off at their mansions, we would review all of the great activities they had just participated in, reminding them of how much fun they had so they would give a glowing report to their parents about their experience at Camp Sheanee.

Through the years, I have frequently thought how different Camp Sheanee is compared to the program our Heavenly Father has designed for us during our lives in mortality, which is a little bit like an extended day camp. I think it's okay with Him if we have a Camp Sheanee experience from time to time, but I doubt He measures our success by how much fun we have in mortality. At the end of the day, I don't think His first question to us will be, "Did you have a good time?" However, many of us think that life should be like Camp Sheanee.

Some of you have either read the writings of, or heard of the great scientist Stephen W. Hawking. He has become one of the greatest minds in physics since Albert Einstein. He remains extremely busy, his work hardly slowed by Lou Gehrig's disease, which has left him completely immobile and unable to speak. For many years he has used a wheelchair and has spoken through a computer and voice synthesizer. He wrote: "I am quite often asked: How do you feel about having ALS? The answer is, not a lot. I try to lead as normal a life as possible, and not think about my condition, or regret the things I cannot do which are not many. . . . I have had motor neurone disease for practically all my adult life, yet it has not prevented me from having a family and being successful in my work."[2]

I am convinced we need never let adversity, whatever form it may take in our individual lives, destroy us or keep us from reaching our potential. The ultimate key to dealing with any kind of adversity is to turn our lives over to God. There really is no other way.

A former secretary of agriculture under President Eisenhower said: "Men and women who turn their lives over to God will discover that he can make a lot more out of their lives than they can. He will comfort their souls, deepen their joys, expand their vision, increase their opportunities, lift their spirits, multiply their blessings, pour out peace, quicken their minds, raise up friends and strengthen their muscles."[3]

All of us will encounter pain and difficulty at some point in our lives. Over twenty years ago, soon after my accident, a colleague of mine quoted to me the following lines from the title of a beautiful little book written by Barbara Johnson: "Pain is inevitable, but misery is optional." How true this is. It is inevitable that we will all have our challenges and obstacles to deal with. However, being miserable over our life and circumstances is optional.

It's like Dr. Beisser writes in his book

> I had to learn to live in the present and discover a way to live with, and hopefully even enjoy, the very limited options which were available to me. I had to discover how to make the most of what came my way. . . . My task was clear—the power to determine how I looked upon life was within me. Whether I considered my disability a great tragedy and a loss or whether I saw it in some more positive light. . . . If this was true . . . new worlds of belief and perception were open to me, and new hope for what my life could be was waiting.[4]

His words echo in my ears and heart each morning as I am dressed in my "outfit" for the day, hoisted out of my bed by a hydraulic patient lifter, transferred to my chair, and quickly reattached to my portable vent. I then get into

a sitting position as opposed to a prone one. Lying in bed I truly feel handicapped, but in my chair, sitting upright, just think of what I can do. I can work on the computer, read and write, or go outside and sit in the sun or roll around, and if I'm real lucky, get hauled into the van and go off with Jo Anne for a never ending adventure. I truly am a lucky—or as I prefer to call it, a blessed man.

Dad / Grandpa / Jack

Notes
1. Arnold R. Beisser, *Flying without Wings*, 135.
2. *Writings of Stephen Hawking*
3. Ezra Taft Benson, *Ensign*, Dec. 1988, 4.
4. Beisser, Ibid., 112, 115.

CONCLUSION

Come What May And
LOVE IT

By Jo Anne Rushton

A WEEK BEFORE Jack's accident, we celebrated our twenty-fifth wedding anniversary. At the writing of this book, I realize that I have been married to Jack for nearly as many years as a quadriplegic as compared to his life before he was hurt.

I will never forget our last moments together before the accident. I was rubbing sunscreen on his back and shoulders, and tender thoughts of our past life together flooded my mind. Then he ran off into the water, and our life was never the same again. Although our life is different now, it is still full of special and wonderful experiences.

I met Jack in my second year of college. As a young, naïve coed, my qualifications for a husband were very high. First, he had to have lots of hair—meaning he couldn't be balding. Second, I didn't want him to wear glasses. I just didn't think they were very attractive. And third, he had to love to dance. I will never forget the first time I heard

Jack speak at a religious service. I was so impressed that I didn't care that he was a little thin on top and wore glasses. The fact that he could dance won me over, and we fell in love.

Before we got married, I visited a church leader who knew Jack very well—probably better than me. As we discussed our upcoming marriage, he looked at me very earnestly and told me that I was marrying the "salt of the earth." Grateful to get such a good man, I never gave the phrase "for better or worse" too much thought. As a new bride, the idea that I might be a caregiver to my husband someday never entered my realm of possibility. For twenty-five years, Jack and I danced our way through life, adjusting our steps to whatever tune was playing at the time.

And then the impossible happened, and we had to learn to dance in a whole new way. I never would have predicted early in Jack's injury that we would be so happy today and find life so pleasant and fulfilling.

I'm grateful the Lord has blessed me with the desire and the ability to care for Jack. It seems so much easier now than it was in the beginning. While I was receiving training for his homecare, I often felt overwhelmed at meeting his many needs, especially the fact that he would be totally dependent on a mechanical respirator for every breath that would go into his lungs. I knew his very life would be in my hands. Many times I would go into the women's restroom at the rehab center and cry. In those moments, I pleaded with the Lord to give me the strength and capacity to do what had to be done so Jack could come home to live. The Lord did bless me, and what I once imagined to be very difficult, and even impossible, is now a way of life.

I have discovered that we can't keep going forward without a sense of humor on both our parts. Once I gave Jack some hot cinnamon mouthwash and forgot I had given it to him. I left the room and did not return until a few minutes later to finally rescue him.

Since the accident, Jack claims he doesn't mind going shopping with me. He says he at least always has somewhere to sit. So when I can't find someone to stay with him, off we go. On one such outing, while I was in the dressing room, Jack was making his way through the aisle and accidentally knocked down several racks of women's lingerie. The sales lady spotted him before he could make his getaway. Fearing she would think he was some kind of weirdo, he tried to explain himself, profusely apologized, and asked her to go and get me. I had to laugh when I finally came to his rescue and saw him sitting there in his wheelchair draped abundantly with ladies undergarments.

Then there was the Christmas morning my youngest daughter, Jackie, and I were hurriedly getting Jack dressed and accidentally rolled him out of bed. Unable to catch him, he ended up on the floor—unharmed, thankfully. It took our neighbor and his four sons-in-law to get him back in bed. Such occasions are funny to us but may look like torture to an onlooker.

Unfortunately, some situations aren't so funny, such as the many close encounters that have nearly cost him his life. Some of the scariest have been when the respirator fails and no one is in earshot.

Jack has had numerous surgeries. During one such episode when he was being prepared for an operation, the anesthesiologist who had been on duty during his last close call recognized him and said, "I know you. You are the miracle man. We almost lost you last time." These kinds of experiences continually remind us that life is a precious gift and ought to be lived to the fullest. Each day is worth remembering.

After Jack's accident, Joseph B. Wirthlin, a prominent leader in our church, told me that it was now my mission to stand by my husband's side and to care for him and to be with him. Wirthlin later said in a special sermon just months before his passing, "Come what may and love it." We have tried to implement this attitude in our lives through the passing years.

Our journey has taken us on a different path than we expected, but it's been an incredible experience, full of blessings, miracles, joy, and oftentimes the unexpected. We truly never know what tomorrow may bring.

I would like to share with you a poem that I feel captures the special relationship that Jack and I share today—all

because I was fortunate enough to marry "the salt of the earth"—hair or not, glasses or not, wheelchair or not.

A Blessed Wife

He may not take me dancing every Friday night,
But we attend church together and try to do what's right.
He may not always whisper sweet nothings in my ear—
But we pray to our Heavenly Father and feel his presence near.
He may not recite Elizabeth Barrett Browning's poetry—
But we always read the scriptures with our dear family.
I may not always be first in his thoughts or in his life—
But being second to God makes me truly a blessed wife.[1]

Note
1. Lola Warren, *Ensign*, Sept. 1997. Revised by Jo Anne Rushton.

Acknowledgments

I DEDICATE THIS selection of observations to my wife, Jo Anne. I also acknowledge that without her love and support over these many years since my accident, I wouldn't be here.

In almost every observation, I refer to her. She is my "straight man" and is such a good sport to let me use her in this way.

Since becoming paralyzed many years, ago I haven't been able to meet any of my physical needs. Jo Anne—with the help of family, friends, and caregivers—has literally kept me alive over the years with never-ending acts of service.

The words I use to describe Jo Anne are "pure gold" and "true grit."

About the Author

JACK RUSHTON IS a respected religious leader and educator who is admired for his leadership skills, devotion to his beliefs and family, and sense of humor. He is now known by thousands for his stellar example of how to move on and continue to achieve fulfillment through service and inspiration, despite unfortunate injuries. Even though Jack is dependent on those around him for most of his physical needs, he still retains the sharp mind and loving spirit that has carried him through his life. All that is Jack remains unchanged.

Jack and his wife, Jo Anne, are the parents of six children and eighteen grandchildren. They reside in Southern California and, in spite of their challenges, truly believe "It's good to be alive!"

To see the book trailer, learn more about the book, or get in touch with the author, please visit www.JackRushton.com.